Educating the Global Citizen

George Walker

Published in 2006 by John Catt Educational Ltd
Great Glemham, Saxmundham, Suffolk IP17 2DH, UK
Tel: +44 (0) 1728 663666 Fax: +44 (0) 1728 663415
E-mail: enquiries@johncatt.co.uk Website: www.johncatt.com

Managing Director: Jonathan Evans. Editor-in-Chief: Derek Bingham

The Sex Discrimination Act of 1975.

The publishers have taken all reasonable steps to avoid a contravention of Section 38 of the Sex Discrimination Act 1975. However, it should be noted that (save where there is an express provision to the contrary) where words have been used which denote the masculine gender only, they shall, pursuant and subject to the said Act, for the purpose of this publication, be deemed to include the feminine gender and *vice versa.*

ISBN: 1 904724 40 X

Set and designed by
John Catt Educational Ltd

Printed and bound in Great Britain by
Bell & Bain Ltd, Glasgow, Scotland

For Jeff Thompson – mentor, colleague and friend.

Contents

Acknowledgements

I want to thank Célia Arcos in the Geneva Headquarters of the International Baccalaureate Organization for her help in preparing the texts of these articles.

I am grateful to my wife, Jenny, and to my colleague, Ian Hill, for reading the articles and suggesting improvements.

Introduction

Education is a national priority, the key to a country's health, wealth and cultural vitality, and all governments have used it as an important lever in achieving their social and economic goals. As recently as a generation ago – say twenty-five years – international education was a niche activity associated with international schools, mobile professional families and students known inelegantly as Third Culture Kids.

Globalization is changing all that. Today no country in the world can ignore events that take place outside its territorial borders. International exchanges, which were rare and exotic a generation ago, are now part of everyday business and family life. Education, which has traditionally preserved and transmitted the values of a particular society, is now changing rapidly to reflect the multicultural nature of a globalized society. International education is revealing an astonishing richness of cultural diversity and, at the same time, addressing some of the tensions that arise from that diversity. It is educating the citizen of the future – the global citizen.

International education encourages both the teacher and the learner to think beyond their own cultural experience. The different knowledge, skills and values that they acquire will help them to become responsible citizens of the world, as well as citizens of their own communities. The two are not incompatible; indeed, to the global citizen, the former is seen as a logical extension of the latter, described by the phrase 'think globally; act locally.'

National education has always contained an international dimension but the need to 'think globally' introduces new concepts and stimulates new interpretations of previous learning. Communication, for example, is no longer satisfactory in a single language. Topics previously viewed from a national perspective become more complex when seen from different but equally legitimate viewpoints. And some of the world's most urgent problems – environmental destruction, poverty and disease – will be solved only through coordinated global action.

International education therefore interrupts 'thinking as usual' as learners realise that other cultures may hold different values, or at least attach different priorities to some of the learner's values; that other groups worship different gods and attach a different significance to their religious beliefs; that other groups reason differently and attach a different meaning even to such fundamental concepts as 'honesty' and 'truth'.

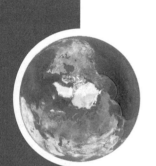

At the heart of international education lies the appreciation of difference, in the sense both of valuing diversity and of calling into question previously unchallenged assumptions and prejudices. At the same time, a stable society can only be constructed from a strong measure of shared understanding and this motivates our search for universal values that will transcend our differences, allowing us to live fulfilled individual lives.

International education therefore introduces an element of complexity, even uncertainty, into the process of learning, both for the teacher and the learner. If, to quote the final sentence of the mission statement of the International Baccalaureate Organization, *'others, with their differences, can also be right'* then those differences must be analyzed, described and accommodated within a new framework of understanding that will necessarily be more complex. International education does not offer global citizens any simple solutions because in truth there will be very few simple solutions in the century ahead, a century that will be characterized by increasing diversity and complexity.

The articles that follow, which were written between 2000 and 2006, when I was director general of the International Baccalaureate Organization, explore in more depth and more detail some of the basic concepts of international education: the apparent tension between human diversity and our common humanity, the importance of intercultural understanding and the search for a set of universal values to unite humankind. In many cases I have tried to indicate some of the implications for teachers who have accepted the daunting responsibility of educating global citizens.

Educating the Global Citizen

You can't remake the world
Without remaking yourself.
Each new year begins within.
It is an inward event,
With unsuspected possibilities
For inner liberation.

(Okri, 1999)

Knowing and understanding

We spend much of our time trying to understand what other people mean, what they are really trying to tell us. Through their actions, what they say, what they write and perhaps even through their appearance: what is it they want us to understand?

Knowing is not the same as understanding when it comes to making sense of the world around us. Knowing stops at information and interest; under-standing implies engagement and you will be familiar with the proverb attributed to Confucius:

'I hear and I forget, I see and I remember, I do and I understand.'

There are many who are content to live their lives on the basis of knowl-edge alone. They can react more quickly, more decisively and often more reassuringly. By contrast, understanding can become a time-consuming business often introducing unwelcome ambiguities, even sometimes ask-ing us to change our minds. But recognizing the difference is important because we are living in an age when to know is no longer enough. The world is shrinking and we can no longer hide, no longer walk away and no longer pretend that someone else's actions do not concern us. We must engage and we must try to understand.

Let me give you two quick examples to illustrate what I mean. During the 1990s, I visited Iraq several times to work at the International School of Baghdad. On one occasion I took a crate of medicines for the Saddam children's hospital. At the border (a rather scary place in the middle of the desert) I was told to report to a doctor who would have to approve the passage of the medicines. He pulled out a random sample of a dozen or so packets and found that one had passed its sell-by date. He shook it at me angrily: "This is out of date and we don't want old pills."

I knew what he meant; he had, after all, said it in perfect English. The single faulty sample had cast a doubt on the quality of the entire load. Moreover he probably took a dim view of this charity and wanted me, from rich, comfortable Switzerland to know it.

"OK," I said, "Then I shall have to leave it here and go on without it, which is a real pity."

"No, no," he replied, "You mustn't do that – but I cannot authorize you to proceed."

At this point, my knowledge began to turn into understanding. Here was this young, articulate doctor (probably trained in the United States) stuck in the middle of nowhere where the temperature was 50° Celsius. He knew that my pathetic offering would make no difference to the children he had seen dying each day in the hospital as a consequence of UN sanctions – perhaps his own children were amongst them. In any case, this was not the way to do business in his country.

It was the doctor who broke the deadlock.

"Can I take some boxes of Aspirin?" he asked.

"Of course you can," I replied and I was immediately waved on my way to Baghdad.

The second example is nearer to my home. A member of the UK upper chamber, the House of Lords, was telling me recently about his experience as a member of a parliamentary commission on global warming. As an historian, he found it astonishing that the distinguished scientists on the commission were unable to agree on the causes of global warming. We all find it convenient to blame the United States for its high profile rejection of the Kyoto Protocol but at the same time we conceal the fact that there remains significant disagreement amongst the scientific community on an issue that has the profoundest consequences for the future of human kind. For the moment, our understanding is partial so the debate must continue.

International education and the global citizen

Going beyond knowing to understanding is a key feature of an international education. You might argue that it should be a key feature of *any* education but my point is that very few issues of significance today can be understood within one's own national context. The situation in Iraq and the phenomenon of global warming affect us all, each provoking different interpretations, different points of view, different possible solutions. The capacity to get under the surface in order to understand these differences, to balance one against another, and to try to resolve them is the hallmark of the global citizen.

I was reminded of this by a pamphlet I received from Washington International School which explains to its parents the school's mission to educate students to be effective and responsible global citizens.

> 'A global citizen is one who seeks out a range of views and perspectives when solving problems. He or she does not "tolerate" or "accept" cultural differences or viewpoints, since these words often implicitly place the speaker at the centre of what is acceptable and right. Global citizens proactively seek out those who have backgrounds that are different from their own, examine ideas that challenge their own, and then *enjoy* the complexity. We must go beyond tolerance and acceptance.'

Two parts of that statement struck me. The first was the reminder that we do indeed put ourselves at the centre of what is acceptable and right. My knowledge, my experience, my culture, these all create lenses through which I focus my understanding of other people and other ideas.

The second point is the reference to *going beyond tolerance* and I was reminded of the comment of the writer E. M. Forster (1951)

> 'Tolerance is a very dull virtue. It is boring. Unlike love, it has always had a bad press. It is negative. It merely means putting up with people, being able to stand things.'

I shall return to this but first I want to explore areas of the school curriculum that I believe will encourage the development of global citizens: young people who are able to

- take themselves away from the centre of what is right and acceptable

- examine the ideas of others that challenge their own beliefs

- go beyond mere tolerance and acceptance

- enjoy the complexity of ambiguity

- nonetheless reach rational conclusions

- in short, have begun to make the transition from knowing to understanding.

I do not start with a blank sheet of paper and I shall not be able to resist the occasional reference to the International Baccalaureate Diploma Programme which, for the sake of brevity, I will refer to simply as 'the IB'. But let me first put on the table Martha Nussbaum's important book, *Cultivating Humanity* (1997) in which she proposes three capacities for developing the humanity which she regards as the essential component of the global citizen in today's world

- a critical examination of oneself and one's traditions

- the ability to see oneself as bound to all other human beings by ties of recognition and concern

- concern and ability to think what it might be like to be in the shoes of a different person.

So let us examine each of these capacities in more depth in the context of a secondary school curriculum and see if we can relate this triangle of academic rigour, human compassion and cultural diversity to the everyday reality of the classroom.

A critical examination of oneself and one's traditions

Very few books in recent years have provoked the interest and the controversy of Dan Brown's *The Da Vinci Code* (2003). I guess the reaction of most people as they reach the end is similar to mine: 'What a great read' followed by 'I wonder if any of it is true?' a question that has spawned a shelf-full of critical analyses. Is it historically accurate, artistically sound, geographically feasible? Does its account of religious schisms contain any religious truth? Is the reader being taken for a ride? Is it fiction or faction?

Don't worry, I am not going to add to the debate, but knowing what is true, and understanding the criteria for judging truth – mathematical, scientific, artistic, religious, moral – lie at the heart of any critical examination. Students must develop reliable benchmarks in their lives against which they can measure themselves and their traditions.

I want to make five very brief curriculum suggestions in order to develop this point.

First, I believe that students should study a broad curriculum while they are at school. It is desirable they engage with the different intellectual methods which humans have devised to make sense of themselves and their surroundings and the excuse 'I find this difficult' is no reason for opting out of it; indeed it could be a good reason for doing more of it, but perhaps differently. In this respect I think the IB offers a good model because it has devised realistic alternatives within learning areas like mathematics and foreign languages, areas which are often deemed to be 'too difficult' for universal study (that is, by anyone who lives outside continental Europe where they are deemed to be essential).

Second, I believe it is especially important that students maintain and develop their studies of the empirical sciences. The social pendulum has swung dramatically from its position when I was at school when scientists were the enviable elite of society: they alone had an explanation of the past and they alone possessed the key to the future. Today, the picture is much more confused and issues like environmental pollution, the nuclear debate, cloning, pharmaceuticals and GM crops provoke angry argument. It is right that they should but let us also remember that science offers a powerful protection against fundamentalism and extremism. It is concerned with observable reality and, refreshingly, makes no claims for eternal truths.

My *third* suggestion is to commend to you the concept of the IB course known as Theory of Knowledge (TOK) which explores questions about different sources and different kinds of knowledge. The following are typical questions for discussion in a TOK lesson:

• Does knowledge come from inside or outside? Do we construct reality or do we recognize it?

• How do computer languages compare with the conventional written and spoken languages of everyday discourse?

• Does the nature of reason vary across cultures?

• Is scientific method a product unique to western culture, or is it universal?

• If truth is difficult to prove in history, does it follow that all versions are equally acceptable?

Students are challenged and often puzzled by TOK, but then they come back five years later to say it was the most important thing they ever did at school.

If TOK is a plus for the IB then my *fourth* observation is a minus. We do not take the study of world religions anything like seriously enough. Indeed, with the exception of a brief appearance in TOK the concepts of religion and spirituality need not appear at all in the IB student's education. I suggest to you that it will become increasingly difficult to make sense of world events without understanding the influence of religious belief on many cultures and, conversely, the influence of cultures upon religious belief.

Fifth, of all the descriptions applied to the IB the one I like best is 'the programme that has the courage to leave the gaps'. Students cannot be expected to cover everything and ensuring the opportunity both for reflection and for digging really deeply into certain parts of their course is surely the sign of a good curriculum. These are both vital aspects of any 'critical examination' as well as being an excellent preparation for university study.

Seeing oneself bound to other human beings

Of all the heart-rending images of the 20th century, few can match the photographs and films of Jewish families being rounded up like cattle, transported in wagons to concentration camps like cattle and then finally slaughtered like cattle. It is the abuse of individual human dignity that is so offensive. That dignity is formally enshrined in our human rights but it is built up from many precious patchwork components: our family and friends, our brief history that is linked to the past and future stories of so many other people, our memories and the memories that others have of us, our ambitions and aspirations. To see all this abused by uniformed thugs in railway sidings and finally destroyed in gas chambers is to see the rejection of any sense of a shared humanity.

We have recently remembered the deaths of 80,000 Japanese civilians when the atom bomb was dropped on Hiroshima 60 years ago. The moral dilemma that this (and other similar actions) poses is obvious and needs addressing. I am not a pacifist and I believe that, in certain extreme situations, war is morally justified, even though one consequence will often be the massive suffering of the innocent. (This does not, of course, imply that all means of pursuing such a war will be justified.) However, the extreme situations that make a war morally defensible must be most carefully defined and scrupulously monitored.

I am labouring this point because I want to counter the argument that war legitimizes any form of violence; that the suicide bomber's calculated slaughter of innocent civilians and of himself is a morally legitimate response to a missile attack which kills innocent civilians. One reason why the war in Iraq has been such a disaster, in my view, is because, launched without United Nations support, it had very dubious legitimacy and that has blurred what was already a very thin, but important, moral line between justifiable and unjustifiable violence against another nation. The deliberate undermining of the Geneva Convention, which is an integral part of a 'just war', has further confused the issue.

The preamble to the 1948 Universal Declaration of Human Rights starts with the words:

> 'Whereas recognition of the inherent dignity and of the equal and inalienable rights of all members of the human family is the foundation of freedom, justice and peace in the world...'

What elements of the curriculum will encourage a sense of belonging to a human family of inherent dignity? What elements of a curriculum might persuade the suicide bomber on the London Underground or the soldier at Srebrenica to change his mind? I am going to make four quick suggestions concerning the curriculum: a woefully inadequate response to such a major challenge but if they encourage you to add more of your own then we shall be getting somewhere.

The *first* will perhaps surprise you, but I believe the recognition of our human artistic potential is a good starting point. One of the best things my parents ever did was to take me to Lascaux in South West France where I saw the fabulous wall paintings several years before the cave was closed for ever. They are breathtaking in their size, colour and vitality but they also provide a profoundly moving human link, a visual response to a human need that leaps across a gap of 17,000 years. The need to draw, to dance and to make music binds us all together and has the power to enhance our dignity.

In May of 2005, European education ministers gathered to commemorate the 60th anniversary of the relief of the Auschwitz concentration camp and they issued a message to the world containing the following recommendation to:

> 'Stress the indispensable and essential value of history teaching for fulfilling the fundamental ambition to educate citizens for the prevention of evil'

and this *second* point reminds me that it was the challenge of history that launched the IB. In 1963 five students at the International School of Geneva took the new Contemporary History examination that offered a more reflective, analytical approach to world history and was the precursor of the IB Diploma Programme five years later. Indeed, the immediate acceptance of one of these candidates by Harvard University provided an important piece of publicity for this new approach to learning.

My *third* point is a very different one because I want to draw attention to the importance of economic understanding. At the most basic level, human dignity is linked to fresh water, food, warmth and shelter. Only when these are satisfied and adequate medical care is available, can human beings begin to achieve their true potential, their true humanity. Huge controversy surrounds current global economics and the institutions that are supposed to exist for the greater good of humanity like the WTO, IMF and the World Bank. Are they good, are they wicked, or are they somewhere in between?

Thomas Friedman's challenging account of globalization in the 21st century (2005) helps us to understand how quickly the economic scene is changing, threatening to turn today's winners, and in particular the United States, into tomorrow's losers, and Friedman encourages us to reflect on the key role that is played by education.

> 'The jobs are going to go where the best educated workforce is with the most competitive infrastructure and environment for creativity and supportive government.'

Today's global citizen therefore needs to understand the main themes that emerge from a modern study of global economics.

My *fourth* point recommends another IB practice, that of community service. The compulsory 'creativity, action, service' programme (known as CAS) is about learning from working alongside others who are not your peers. It does not pretend to be a substitute for social service, though on occasions it may become that, but rather it aims to challenge the student to think about the lessons learned from an experience that brings them into contact with other people in a way that may be radically different from day-to-day life at school. It is an essential component of the course and without its satisfactory completion, the student will not gain the IB diploma.

Wearing the shoes of a different person

Much has been written about the capacity to identify with someone else's culture and I have myself cautioned against some of the overambitious claims that have been made, especially by international schools (see page

27). Nonetheless, I think we can all readily agree that the capacity to empathize, or at the very least to see the other person's point of view, is essential for the global citizen. If culture really is the 'software of the mind', as Geert Hofstede has famously suggested (1991), then it is going to require a special effort to re-route the cultural wiring that we seem to have acquired by the end of primary schooling; it will not happen by chance.

I cannot resist a minor diversion at this point in order to illustrate how that wiring is sometimes laid down. A friend has recently sent me an hilarious book entitled *The Clumsiest People in Europe* (Pruzan, 2005) which is an edited reprint of three short books written around 1850 by a famous English children's writer, Mrs Favell Lee Mortimer. Mrs Mortimer only left England twice during her lifetime, once for Paris and Brussels and once for Edinburgh, but that did not stop her expressing her extensive views on the cultural characteristics of diverse nations around the world. You can anticipate her comments about Australia's aboriginal people:

'The savages of Australia have neither god, nor king'

but those closer to her home, with white skins and a decent job to go to, do not seem to have impressed her any better. For example:

'Nothing useful is well done in Sweden.'

It is tempting to laugh at Mrs Mortimer's poisonous comments (prefaced by the reminder: *'Which country do you love best? Your **own** country.'*) until we remember that, as a best-selling children's author, she had a huge influence on the cultural attitudes of young people in Victorian England. Nor should we suppose that the cultural stereotypes that she helped to create have entirely disappeared 150 years later.

What contribution can the curriculum make to a young person's sensitivity to cultural difference? I have time for only two suggestions and each of them deserves a lecture of its own.

Let me start with the great American psychologist, Jerome Bruner (1996), who has suggested that all cultures organize their knowledge of the world into two broad and distinctive ways: as logical scientific and as narrative thinking. I spoke earlier of the importance of science, not just for its economic benefits, but also as a bastion against extremism. Let me now look in more detail at the narrative expression of culture.

The IB puts great emphasis on the study of literature, both in the mother tongue and in translation from other languages. Literature is a powerful medium for exploring the influence of culture and I defy anyone, for example, to be unmoved by J. M. Coetzee's, early novel *Waiting for the Barbarians* (1980) and its stark description of total cultural separation in the defence of a doomed empire. It was, of course, a parable for the apartheid regime in South Africa.

A friend told me recently that she was unable to finish Chimamanda Adichie's novel, *Purple Hibiscus* (2004), because she found it too upsetting. Certainly the portrayal of the domineering Nigerian father as democrat, fanatical catholic convert and child abuser is profoundly disturbing. But the book is really about the impact of confused cultural messages on the impressionable teenager, Kambili: a destabilizing mixture of British imperial legacy, the catholic church and Nigerian tribal tradition.

Let me recommend two other books that have similarly impressed me by their handling of cultural difference. The first is the remarkable novel by the Turkish writer, Orhan Pamuk, *My Name is Red* (2001) which is set in late 16th century Istanbul. It really does force you to try on different shoes because the same events are observed, chapter by chapter, by different people – even a dog and a horse make their own contributions – and the reader is conscious of being immersed in a quite different cultural context. Finally, my favourite book of the last decade is *Le Testament Français* by the Russian novelist, Andrei Makine (1997), which explores the cultural ambiguity experienced by a boy growing up with his French grandmother in the Soviet Union in the 1980s. It is a wonderful book with a very sharp sting in its tail.

I have no idea if the books I have just mentioned are included in the IB world literature list and it does not matter because there are ten more like them for every one I have mentioned. My point is that, in the hands of a good teacher, literature is a very powerful medium for exploring the importance of culture and for understanding the consequences of cultural difference.

Language is an integral part of culture but I am afraid I do not accept the argument that the study at school of a foreign language will throw open the door to new cultures – though later on it might. Let us be less ambitious, more realistic and accept that a new language will extend the student's range of communication and crucially will demonstrate a willingness to pay homage to another culture, to move oneself from the centre of what is right and to put oneself at a profound disadvantage. I know from the day-to-day experience of living in a French-speaking community just how much of yourself is surrendered when you are required to communicate in another language. Quite simply, you have abandoned part of yourself and assumed a different and more defensive identity.

I have reached my final point which is perhaps the toughest of all. Shortly after the London bombings of 7 July 2005, I read an over-hasty article in the UK *Sunday Times* by Michael Portillo (2005), a former Conservative minister and a member of the intellectual Right, entitled 'Multiculturalism has failed but tolerance can save us'. The article rejected multiculturalism as the appropriate model for accommodating ethnic minorities in Britain (particularly in its newly terrorised condition) but based this conclusion on a fundamentally wrong definition of multiculturalism – in my view – namely that all cultures are equal in value.

I see no reason to suppose that all cultures are equal in value, either in an intrinsic or a pragmatic sense. The pragmatic point is obvious enough: cultures must change with their environment and the capacity of some to survive, except as protected species, in an increasingly globalized society must be in doubt in the long term. However, it is more controversial to suggest that some cultures are intrinsically less valuable than others but if they encourage oppression, mysticism and ignorance; if they prevent human beings, particularly women, from achieving their full potential, then I believe that is a justifiable conclusion. The global citizen has to make choices and to account for them. I well remember an alumnus of the International School of Geneva telling me that the school had left him with an overwhelming burden of tolerance; it had never helped him to decide where to draw the line and how to say about any practice 'I find that unacceptable'.

Can we therefore look at the term 'multicultural' from a different angle, applying it to individual members of a society, rather than to the society as a whole? Can we ask how global citizens might become multicultural; how they might respond to another culture not only to enrich their own lives, but to indicate their respect and openness towards others, in a minority, in their society? It could be in trivial ways by eating different food or in profound ways through the choice of a partner. It might be by embracing another culture's music, its films and its literature. It could be by learning another culture's language or by taking a job that involves daily contact with a very different group of people.

This is what the Lebanese/French writer, Amin Maalouf (2000), calls the 'thread of affiliation':

'A "thread of affiliation" links me to the crowd: the thread may be thick or thin, strong or weak, but it is easily recognisable by all those who are sensitive on the subject of identity.'

I believe that global citizens want to try to create these cultural threads of affiliation between themselves and those around them.

I have exhausted my time and probably exhausted your patience. I have been trying to emphasize the combination of three qualities in the global citizen: intellectual rigour, human compassion and cultural sensitivity. Let me therefore end with a brief statement, the IBO mission statement, which I hope encapsulates all three:

'The International Baccalaureate Organization aims to develop inquiring, knowledgeable and caring young people who help to create a better and more peaceful world through intercultural understanding and respect.

'To this end the IBO works with schools, governments and international organizations to develop challenging programmes of international education and rigorous assessment.

'These programmes encourage students across the world to become active, compassionate and lifelong learners who understand that other people, with their differences, can also be right.'

Tenth biennial conference of the Association of Heads of Independent Schools of Australia, Adelaide, September 2005

References

Adichie, C (2004) *Purple Hibiscus*. Harper Perennial.

Brown, D (2003) *The Da Vinci Code*. Doubleday.

Bruner, J (1996) *The Culture of Education*. Harvard UP.

Coetzee, J M (1980) *Waiting for the Barbarians*. Secker and Warburg.

Forster, E M (1951) Tolerance. *Two Cheers for Democracy*. Arnold.

Friedman, T (2005) *The World is Flat*. Allen Lane.

Hofstede, G (1991) *Cultures and Organizations*. McGraw-Hill.

Maalouf, A (2000) *In the name of identity: violence and the need to belong*. Arcade Publishing.

Makine, A (1997) *Le Testament Français.* Hodder & Stoughton.

Nussbaum, M (1997) *Cultivating Humanity.* Harvard UP.

Okri, B (1999) *Turn on your light.* Phoenix House.

Pamuk, O (2001) *My Name is Red.* Faber & Faber.

Portillo, M (2005) *Multiculturalism has failed but tolerance can save us. Sunday Times.* 17th July.

Pruzan, T (Ed) (2005) *The Clumsiest People in Europe.* Bloomsbury.

"Education, which has traditionally preserved and transmitted the values of a particular society, is now changing rapidly to reflect the multicultural nature of a globalized society."

Understanding what a culture is, and why it is so important in determining our relationship with other people are key elements of global citizenship. If I am to respect someone else's culture then I must both understand and respect my own.

The next two articles explore different aspects of cultural understanding.

'One-way streets of our culture' borrows as its title a phrase from the eminent American psychologist, Jerome Bruner, and it examines critically some of the claims made by international educators about the ease of standing in another person's cultural shoes.

'Joseph Conrad: international narrator' pays tribute to a man who could serve as a role-model for the global citizen. It also illustrates the way in which well-chosen literature can enhance our cultural understanding with an analysis of three of Conrad's short stories.

One-way streets of our culture

When distinctions are drawn between international education and education in general, the phrase 'cultural understanding' is never far away; indeed it plays a key part in most descriptions and justifications of international education. The study of Hayden and Thompson (1996) confirms that students and teachers perceive mixing with those of different cultures to be a core element in international education and this gives substance to an act of faith long held and promoted by international schools. But many of these schools claim to do more than just encourage the 'rubbing of shoulders'. The deliberate, planned integration of students from different cultural backgrounds is widely regarded as a cornerstone of international education.

The charter of the world's oldest international school (the International School of Geneva) commits it to the ambitious aim of the 'preparation of students for the reintegration into their own cultures or for integration into other cultures'. Renaud, writing in Jonietz and Harris (1991), asserts that the mission of all international schools is 'to prepare young people – the decision makers of tomorrow – to live in a complex multicultural society'. Leach (1969), in the earliest book about international schools, expresses the hope that international school students will 'find themselves "at home" in all cultures and human situations'.

However, experienced international educators disagree on whether these ambitious aims can be achieved. Whilst Belle-Isle (1986) writes encouragingly about 'the cultural mobility not only of the individual but most of all of thought', Mattern, writing in Jonietz and Harris (1991), is more cautious and wonders if anyone 'will be able to stand wholly comfortably in the shoes of a culture different from one's own'. Renaud (1995) recognizes the problem when he suggests 'what we call international understanding rarely gets underneath the surface and may even be paternalistic', but how realistic is his insistence that 'we must go further and deeper, really to grasp another person's values'.

It is not surprising that we also find disagreement about the best ways of achieving cultural understanding. In what is probably the earliest, and certainly the most uncompromising, description of international education, Maurette (1948) insists that 'although it is wrong to attempt to "denationalize" students, a study of their own culture can be justified only as an enrichment of an international perspective to which it should be "clearly subordinated"'. Belle-Isle, quoted by Renaud (1995), takes the opposite view, arguing that a young person's self-awareness starts from an understanding of her or his own cultural values, and Peterson's (1987) account of the interlinked origins of the United World Colleges and the International Baccalaureate Organization reminds us that both worked from the basic premise that students must have one foot firmly planted in their own culture before trying to step out into another.

It is thus apparent that some of the claims made by international educators are contradictory while others might be considered simplistic, given the cultural complexity of a typical international school, the mobile and transient nature of many of its students and the powerful influence of the school's own culture.

This paper explores some meanings of the term 'culture'; precisely what it is that we are helping students to understand when we speak about 'cultural understanding'? It also proposes ways in which international schools can help their students to learn about other cultures and perhaps avoid becoming trapped, in Bruner's (1983) memorable phrase, in the 'one-way streets created by our culture'.

Definitions of culture

T. S. Eliot (1948) defined culture as 'the way of life of a particular people living together in one place… made visible in their arts, social system, in their habits and customs, in their religion' and insisted, in uncompromising relativist mood, that 'the culture of a people is the incarnation of its religion' and (of Britain) 'if Christianity goes, the whole of our culture goes'. His second statement takes most international educators beyond their comfort zone and issues related to religious differences are usually swept with some embarrassment under the international school carpet. Yet if cultural understanding, leading perhaps to greater cultural empathy, is to have any meaning, we cannot ignore this fundamental dimension of human experience.

Belle-Isle (1986) notes: 'It is sometimes said that international education should avoid such sensitive subjects as race, religion and origin. On the contrary, however, it seems to me that the common denominator of international education must arise from the variety of religions, races and origins – that is to say, from the rich diversity of the cultural heritage of a boundless world.' Belle-Isle does not explain how this cultural common denominator might arise but he is surely right in implying that the search may be tough and uncomfortable. An honest study of why a group of apparently decent, rational people should, under certain conditions, torture, rape and murder a neighbouring group of apparently decent, rational people may cause some offence. However, the international educator cannot avoid the controversial issues that often underlie cultural priorities, but must explore them in a debate characterized, in Belle-Isle's words, by knowledge, open-mindedness and dignity.

In an essay that explores the interaction between the powers of individual minds and the means by which culture aids or thwarts their realization, Bruner (1996) proposes ways in which teachers can develop cultural understanding. He reminds the reader that there are often widely different ways of looking at the same thing; meanings vary according to the cultural context and within a particular culture there will sometimes be official meanings that are not open to challenge. Education can ensure that those canonical interpretations are scrutinized and thereby encourage the culture to adapt to change. 'Deciding whether or not to accept this challenge', writes Bruner, 'is what makes [education] either a somewhat dangerous pursuit or a rather drearily routine one.'

Belle-Isle's attempt to identify cultural common denominators belongs to a wider search for a universally applicable set of values that will bind together peoples of different cultures. Mattern, for example, writing in Jonietz and Harris (1991), states that there are 'certain values... which are, and have been, common to every civilization past and present'. However, there is still little evidence that a global sharing of even the basic values of '*liberté, égalité et fraternité*' engages people at the deepest emotional level. On the contrary, the increasing number of nation states, the celebration of linguistic differences, the growth of ethnic awareness and the protection of minority groups suggest that the common denominator approach to culture is too simplistic.

A community's response to its particular environmental situation will cause it to develop a set of cultural values which will help to protect it and to strengthen its chances of survival. Only when it is confronted by issues that pose a wider threat – environmental damage, weapons of mass destruction or epidemic disease, for example – will the community perceive the merits of adopting a wider set of cultural values in order to strengthen its chances of survival. This observation is hardly new: it was explored by Rousseau in the eighteenth century and it underpins the entire structure of the United Nations and its associated organs of world government.

Hofstede (1991) has approached the question of a shared culture from a different perspective. He has described culture as the 'software of the mind'; it is a community's culture that translates a set of experiences, many of them symbolically encoded, into shared meaning. Hofstede illustrates his definition with a layered, onion-like model that locates cultural practices (symbols, heroes and rituals) near the surface and the values that they represent embedded in the centre. It is the deeply held values of a community, its 'broad tendencies to prefer certain states of affairs over others', that characterize its culture.

Hofstede's research, which has been broadly confirmed by others in the field, suggests that all cultures are confronted by a limited number of basic social challenges. These are: uneven distribution of power, the relationship between the individual and the group, concepts of masculinity and femininity, and ways of handling uncertainty. It is their distinctly different responses to these common problems that distinguish different cultural groups. The implications for teachers in a multicultural school are considerable. A French child, for example, from a cultural background that regards ambiguity as unsettling, is unlikely to respect the American science teacher who looks down her microscope and announces with total confidence to the entire class, 'I have no idea what is going on here!' Japanese parents, from a cultural background in which social gender roles are distinct, are much more likely than, for example, Scandinavian parents to take a very serious view of their son's failure at school.

The work of Hofstede and others who are exploring how different cultural communities think, feel and act, had its origins in the multinational world of commerce where companies routinely expect multicultural teams to work together to solve important corporate problems. It is now beginning to attract attention from international educators such as Cambridge, writing in Hayden and Thompson (1998), who are asking how the cultural unity that has traditionally been associated with the 'effective school' can be reconciled with the cultural diversity that is the norm of the international school.

The Director-General of UNESCO, Federico Mayor (1998), has insisted that 'creative rebellion is essential in order to open up the paths to the future'. If Mayor is right that 'it is solely with energy, non-violent protest and a willingness to take risks' that we can meet the challenges of the modern world, we may begin to understand from Hofstede's research why some cultures seem unable to participate on an equal footing with others in the transmission of new values, and especially those that lead to rapid economic growth.

Culture and the international school

A shared culture is, according to Eliot, 'what makes life worth living' because it enables members of a group to share their understanding of the world. But it is also a powerful mechanism for legitimizing acceptable forms of behaviour within that group. A culture is a means of control and this is what makes teaching (especially in an international school) a rather risky activity because, in Stenhouse's words (1967), 'the object of education is to make culture more a resource and less a determinant'; it is 'preeminently the task of education so to induct people into culture that their personal freedoms are preserved and indeed enhanced'.

Stenhouse emphasizes the importance of language in this process: '[language] becomes the possession of the individual, who can, as it were, carry it with him into his inner privacy and use it as an instrument of thought. True individuality derives from such reflection'. Without appropriate language, a young person is barred from his own and from another's culture. Nothing indicates a school's commitment to an international education more clearly than the level of resources that it is prepared to devote to the teaching of languages.

However, since resources are finite, it will be necessary to establish priorities. Which is to be deemed the most important in the development of cultural awareness:

- fluency in the language(s) of instruction, which provides the key to the student's active participation in the process of learning?

- the acquisition of a new language, which will widen the student's cultural horizon, particularly if it is the language of the surrounding environment?

- maintaining the student's mother tongue, which will encourage the strong growth of that student's cultural identity?

Although most international schools can be described as 'multicultural' in terms of their student population and sometimes in terms of their staff, the style of learning that they encourage is overwhelmingly in the tradition of Western liberal humanism. This is further reinforced by the origins and nature of the membership organizations, examination systems and accrediting agencies that have supported the rapid development of international education. Lawton (1998) has described how the modern multicultural society permits cultural minorities to express themselves only in 'the context of a more or less Christian influenced, post-Christian, humanist, rationalist environment'. Those who belong to the majority culture may, from time to time, glimpse significantly different ways of looking at the world, but it requires an unusually gifted faculty of teachers to offer practical ways of redressing this powerful bias.

Bruner addresses this inequality with three proposals. First, an international school should be a place where learners support each other in an active environment where the different cultural contributions become an asset, thus enriching the Western pedagogical tradition which (despite its liberalism and humanism) has tended to favour a one-way transmission model of knowledge from the teacher to the student.

Second, the mobility of students, which is the *raison d'être* of the international school, gives an additional significance to the creation of external works, '*oeuvres*' as Bruner calls them, which represent collective cultural activity and create an enduring record of otherwise invisible mental effort. The concert, the drama production, science fair, simulated United Nations, the yearbook, poetry anthology: these are all examples of such oeuvres, and they are especially relevant to international education because they represent the tangible evidence of cultural understanding. The potential of electronic mail in maintaining contact and building records of learning amongst transient international populations is only just being exploited.

Finally, Bruner notes how all cultures organize their knowledge of the world in two broad and distinctive ways: as logical scientific and as narrative thinking. Different cultures attribute a different status to each but, he insists, our understanding of our cultural origins is framed in story form. The creation of narrative sensibility is as important for the structuring of individual life as it is for the cohesion of a culture as a whole. This means that the arts of narrative – music, drama, fiction, theatre – will be especially important in international education, both to help mobile children feel at home in the world and to aid the process of exploring, and thereby better understanding, cultural differences.

Conclusion

Modern travel and communication have created the metaphor of the global village. But distinct cultural identities remain strong and amongst many groups they are being deliberately encouraged and strengthened. International education must help students to understand what is meant by culture, first in relation to their own national identity and then – in a process based on knowledge, open-mindedness and dignity – in relation to the traditions of others. They will come to understand how:

- a truly shared meaning depends upon a shared culture;

- a culture develops a protective mechanism which will intensify when the group is threatened;

- changes in culture will follow changes in the external environment and especially when new (*eg* global) threats have been clearly perceived;

- language, especially the mother tongue, plays a key role in understanding and developing a culture;

- a culture reflects a group's values and is therefore a powerful means of social control;

- a limited number of fundamental social problems seems to confront every culture, but the responses to these problems are culturally differentiated;

- international schools are dominated by a Western liberal, humanist culture;

- teachers cannot escape the dilemma of sometimes supporting and sometimes challenging a set of cultural values;

- certain styles of learning seem to be especially suited to developing cultural understanding.

Although international educators will reject the extreme position of the cultural relativists, who insist that understanding another culture is simply not possible within the context of one's own culture, they would be wise to avoid making overambitious claims. Instead, they might take a lead from the more modest observation of Roger Peel (1998), who writes of the International Baccalaureate:

'It is not expected that students adopt alien points of view, merely that they are exposed to them and encouraged to respond intelligently. The end result, we hope, is a more compassionate population, a welcome manifestation of national diversity within an international framework of tolerant respect.'

Reprinted by permission of Peridot Press from
International Schools Journal Vol XIX No. 2 © Peridot Press, 2000

References

Belle-Isle, R. (1986) Learning for a new humanism. *International Schools Journal.* 11. 27-30.

Bruner, J. S. (1996) *The Culture of Education.* Cambridge, MA: Harvard University Press.

Bruner, J. S. (1983) *In Search of Mind.* London: Harper & Row.

Eliot, T. S. (1948) *Notes Towards the Definition of Culture.* London: Faber & Faber.

Hayden, M. C. & Thompson J. J. (1996) (Eds) Potential difference: the driving force for international education. *International Schools Journal.* XVI (1). 46-57.

Hayden, M. C. & Thompson J. J. (1998) (Eds) *International Education – Principles and Practice.* London: Kogan Page.

Hofstede, G. (1991) *Cultures and Organisations.* McGraw-Hill.

International School of Geneva (1990) *Charter and Regulations.*

Jonietz, P. L. & Harris N. D. C. (Eds) (1991) *World Yearbook of Education.* London: Pergamon Press.

Lawton, C. (1998) Is multiculturalism cultural oppression? *International School (is).* 1 (1). 10.

Leach, R. J. (1969) *International Schools and their Role in the Field of International Education.* London: Pergamon Press.

Maurette, M-T. (1948) *Educational Techniques for Peace.* UNESCO.

Mayor, F. (1998) *Address to Intercontinental Congress on Education.* UNESCO.

Peel, R. (1998) *Education for Life.* Geneva: International Baccalaureate Organization.

Peterson, A. D. C. (1987) *Schools Across Frontiers.* Chicago, IL: Open Court Publishing Co.

Renaud, O. (1995) *Address to Annual Conference of International Schools Association.*

Stenhouse, L. (1967) *Culture and Education.* Walton-on-Thames: Thomas Nelson.

Joseph Conrad: international narrator

Introduction

Cultural awareness – the capacity to identify significant components of a culture, to understand how culture programmes behaviour and to respect cultural diversity – lies at the heart of international education. Thirty years ago the General Conference of UNESCO (1974) meeting in Paris adopted a recommendation which urged all its member states to accept as a guiding principle for international education 'understanding and respect for all peoples, their cultures, civilizations, values and ways of life' and 10 years ago (IBE, 1994), at the International Conference on Education in Geneva, the world's ministers of education drew attention to the importance of 'educating caring and responsible citizens, open to other cultures'.

The mission statement of the International Baccalaureate Organization (IBO, 2002) quotes its aim as 'to develop inquiring, knowledgeable and caring young people who help create a better and more peaceful world through intercultural understanding and respect'. Hill (2002), reflecting on an earlier mission statement, believes that 'only when students a capable of "respecting the variety of cultures and attitudes that makes for the richness of life" will the possibility of establishing an ideology in international education exist'. Studies by Hayden and Thompson (1995) confirm that those who have received an international education perceive cultural awareness as a key element, an opinion summed up by a university student who wrote: 'I still have my own set of values and am still greatly influenced by my culture, but I don't expect everyone to be like me, to believe in everything I believe in.'

I have drawn attention (Walker, 2000 or page 25 of this book) to the overambitious cultural claims that are sometimes made on behalf of international education which, it has been variously suggested, will 'prepare students for integration into another culture', enable students 'to find themselves at home in all cultures and human situations', and help them to 'grasp another person's values'. An earlier director general of the IBO (Peel, 1998) has proposed more modestly that 'it is not expected that students adopt alien points of view, merely that they are exposed to them and encouraged to respond intelligently'.

Organizing the exposure and encouraging the intelligent response is therefore a particular challenge for the international educator, one that can be approached through a variety of different pedagogical strategies. The eminent developmental psychologist, Jerome Bruner (1996), has suggested that the narrative arts – music, drama, fiction, theatre – have special roles to play in exploring cultural differences and this is reflected for example, in the IBO's insistence on world literature as a compulsory element of its mother-tongue language courses. World literature:

> '… does not aim to equip students with a 'mastery' of other cultures. It is envisaged as having the potential to enrich the international awareness of students and to develop in them the attitudes of tolerance, empathy and genuine respect for perspectives different from their own.' (IBO, 1999)

Some authors, because of the richness of their own cultural experiences, coupled with their power to communicate them through their stories, have a very special contribution to make in this respect. Such a writer is Joseph Conrad.

A major novelist

Conrad was born Józéf Teodor Konrad Korzeniowski in 1857. His mother tongue was Polish, which he spoke fluently throughout his life. At the age of five he learned French, which he always spoke accurately and without an accent. When he came to write fiction, however, he wrote in English, a language he had not met until the age of 20.

Conrad was born in Berdyczów in the Polish Ukraine which had long been annexed by Russia. At the age of four he was taken by his parents from Warsaw to Vologda, 500 kilometres north of Moscow, where his father had been exiled as punishment for his political activities. His mother died when he was seven, leaving him in the care of his literary-minded father, who died four years later. Conrad then came increasingly under the influence of a maternal uncle with whom he enjoyed a close, if sometimes turbulent, relationship until the latter's death in 1894.

In 1874, against his uncle's wishes, Conrad joined the French merchant navy and four years later transferred to the British merchant navy where he served for the next 16 years, taking regular examinations and gaining steady promotion until he achieved his own command. His first novel, *Almayer's Folly*, was written in his last years at sea and was published in 1895. By now living in England, he produced a series of novels and short stories, each costing him heavily in terms of his health, culminating in 1914 with his only commercial success, the novel *Chance*. The final decade of his life failed to provide the inspiration of his earlier masterpieces: H*eart of Darkness* (1899),

Lord Jim (1900), *Nostromo* (1904) and *The Secret Agent* (1907). Conrad died near Canterbury in south-east England in 1924.

Conrad's reputation as a major writer was slow to develop and it was another quarter of a century before the eminent critic, F. R. Leavis, welcomed him into the pantheon of major English writers:

> 'The great English novelists are Jane Austen, George Eliot, Henry James and Joseph Conrad, major novelists who count in the same way as the major poets, in the sense that they not only change the possibilities of the art for practitioners and readers, but that they are significant in terms of the human awareness they promote: awareness of the possibilities of life.' (Leavis, 1948: 9)

A global nomad

Joseph Conrad's early life contains many of the features that we now associate with the 'global nomad' (Langford, 1998). His childhood was seriously disrupted by his parents' exile and their early deaths and he rejected the home that was offered by his uncle, choosing instead to travel the world, a decision that caused him guilt for the rest of his life:

> 'I catch myself in hours of solitude and retrospect meeting arguments and charges made thirty-five years ago by voices now forever still; finding things to say that an assailed boy could not have found, simply because of the mysteriousness of his impulses to himself. I understood no more than the people who called upon me to explain myself.' (Conrad, 1988: 118)

As a sailor he criss-crossed the globe, witnessing the events and meeting the people that would later enrich his novels, particularly those set in the Far East. His experience of the navy also provided an important stability in his early life not unlike that offered by the international school in the lives of young global nomads today. Looking back, he wrote: 'The Red Ensign – the symbolic, protecting, warm bit of bunting flung wide upon the seas, and destined to be the only roof over my head' (Conrad, 1988: 135). Conrad was multilingual but he was never in any doubt why he wrote his fiction in his third language, English:

> 'I have a strange and overpowering feeling that it had always been an inherent part of myself. English was for me neither a matter of choice or of adoption. The merest idea of choice had never entered my head.' (Conrad, 1988: author's note)

He took British nationality in 1886 and, although he always expressed his affection and admiration for his adopted country and tried in his last years to acquire the style of an English country squire, he was always uncomfortably conscious of not being English. In 1903, in a letter to a Polish historian (Knowles and Moore, 2001: 117) he defined himself as '*homo duplex*': 'Both at sea and on land my point of view is English from which the conclusion should not be drawn that I have become an Englishman. This is not the case.' Even when he had 'settled' in England, Conrad moved house eight times and despite acquiring social respectability and some wealth he never owned his own property. He turned down the offer of honorary degrees from several British universities and in 1924 refused a knighthood from the British Prime Minister. Instead, he waited for the international recognition of the Nobel Prize for Literature, but in vain.

Perhaps most revealingly, H. G. Wells (Baines, 1960: 234) describes a scene in which Conrad had completely misinterpreted a light-hearted remark by George Bernard Shaw: 'One could always baffle Conrad by saying "humour". It was one of our damned English tricks he had never learned to tackle', and when Virginia Woolf wrote his obituary in August 1924, she referred to Conrad, despite his 30 years' residence in England, as 'our guest' (Knowles and Moore, 2001: 117). He had never really belonged.

Making us see

Given these personal circumstances, it is unsurprising that the themes of cultural dissonance and cultural isolation play a prominent role in Conrad's writing. In *Lord Jim*, for example, the eponymous hero, son of a middle class English vicar, wanders ever further east seeking atonement for a youthful error of judgement, finally becoming leader of an isolated tribe in Patustan (Indonesia). Conrad writes from personal experience of the isolation of exile:

> 'Each blade of grass has a spot on earth whence it draws its life, its strength; and so is man rooted to the land from which he draws his faith together with his life.' (Baines, 1960: 401)

It is in this novel, incidentally, that Conrad creates the culturally defining phrase: 'He was one of us'.

Charles Gould, owner of the silver mine that drives Conrad's greatest novel, *Nostromo*, is portrayed as an aloof English country gentleman, unable to recognize the growing irrelevance of the values of his English education to the deteriorating situation in the revolutionary state of Costaguana. In *The Secret Agent*, Adolf Verloc is part of an underground network of terrorism involving embassies, the police and various anarchist groups but in reality he is totally isolated from them all, and from his English wife who eventually murders him. Best known of all is the cultural shock experienced by the ivory trader, Kurtz, in *Heart of Darkness*, which leads to his moral collapse and to Conrad's enduring words: 'The horror! The horror!' Once again, Conrad is writing from personal experience about the disorienting effect of unfamiliar, hostile surroundings: 'I think (the wilderness) had whispered to him things about himself which he did not know, things of which he had no conception until he took counsel with his great solitude' (Conrad, 2002a: 164).

Conrad believed he had a social role to play as a writer:

> 'I would not like to be left standing as a mere spectator on the bank of a great stream carrying onward many lives. I would fain claim for myself the faculty of so much insight as can be expressed in a voice of sympathy and compassion.' (Conrad, 1988: 5)

He did not want to judge, but rather to explain and to clarify: 'My task which I am trying to achieve is, by the power of the written word to make you hear, to make you feel – it is, before all, to make you see' (Conrad, 1963: 13), and, as we shall see later, he adopted particular narrative techniques to help to build a special relationship between himself and his reader.

Conrad wrote 19 short stories between 1896 and 1916 and some of his longer novels, even the epic *Nostromo*, were first conceived in that form. It seemed to suit him, giving a test bed for experimentation, a welcome relief from the struggle of longer writing and much needed cash from magazines of the day such as *Blackwood's, Pall Mall Magazine* and the *Illustrated London News*.

In the three stories described here, Conrad explores several aspects of cultural awareness: the difficulty of comprehending events that take place outside a shared cultural framework, the possibility of understanding a different set of cultural values and the social exclusion of minority cultural groups.

The outpost of progress

Conrad acknowledged (1928: author's note) that 'An Outpost of Progress' had the same origin as *Heart of Darkness*: his journey up the Congo River in 1890 that had undermined his health. Although in some ways a proto-type for the more famous story, it is also an outstanding example of tight-ly written irony (starting with its title) and was a favourite of the author (Knowles and Moore, 2001: 301).

Two Belgians, Kayerts, a former civil servant, and Carlier, a former sol-dier, are left to run an ivory trading station deep in the African jungle. 'For days the two pioneers of trade and progress would look on their empty courtyard in the vibrating brilliance of vertical sunshine' (Conrad, 1997: 8). They become increasingly aware of their own inex-perience and vulnerability in the midst of a dangerously alien environ-ment 'Few men realise that their life, the very essence of their charac-ter, their capabilities and their audacities, are only the expression of their belief in the safety of their surroundings.' (p. 5)

Kayerts and Carlier have no understanding of their surroundings, which contain nothing to which they can connect their earlier existence:

> 'And stretching away in all directions, surrounding the insignifi-cant cleared spot of the trading post, immense forests, hiding fate-ful complications of fantastic life, lay in the eloquent silence of mute greatness. The two men understood nothing, cared for noth-ing but for the passage of days that separated them from the steamer's return.' (p. 8)

Each is terrified lest the other should die, leaving him to survive on his own, so the climax brings the ultimate irony when, after a quarrel over their dwindling reserves of food, Kayerts accidentally shoots Carlier and, realizing what he has done, hangs himself just hours before the company steamer arrives to relieve the station.

Kayerts and Carlier have been cut off from their White cultural life sup-port system. They have no understanding of the Africans upon whom they ultimately depend and are only able to perceive them in terms of western stereotypes, for example, as potential cavalry soldiers. But they also have less and less understanding of each other and, despite their physical close-ness and mutual dependence, each lives in a state of growing isolation, separated from all the shared understandings that make true communica-tion possible:

> 'They believed their words. Everyone shows a respectful defer-ence to certain sounds that he and his fellows can make. But about feelings people really know nothing. We talk with indigna-

tion or enthusiasm; we talk about oppression, cruelty, crime, devotion, self-sacrifice, virtue, and we know nothing real beyond the words.' (p. 15)

By the end of the tale, the idea of White Europeans bringing 'progress' to Africa seems laughable. This was a brave story to publish in 1897. It was the year of Queen Victoria's Diamond Jubilee, which made the story's theme particularly provocative, and alongside the first instalment the magazine *Cosmopolis* ran an article extolling the economic, military and territorial virtues of her long reign.

'Karain: A Memory'

Both the tone and the style of the opening words of the short story 'Karain: A Memory', published a year later, signal a significant change in Conrad's writing. 'We knew him in those unprotected days when we were content to hold in our hands our lives and our property' (Conrad, 1997: 36). The author is no longer speaking directly to the reader. For the first time, Conrad has appointed a narrator to tell the tale, creating a device that he would use in many of his later novels, most notably *Heart of Darkness*, *Lord Jim* and *Chance*, all of which feature the retired sailor, Conrad's fictional double, Marlow.

In using a first-person narrator, Conrad has abandoned the omniscient third-person narrative of 'An Outpost of Progress'. He is inviting the reader to listen to the narrator, as others are presumably doing, and to make up his own mind about the story. It is the author's way of encouraging the reader's participation and it also allows Conrad to explore points of view that he would not necessarily hold himself but would come more naturally from the mouth of the narrator.

In 'Karain', the narrator is the entrepreneurial skipper of a ship that is illegally supplying arms to a tiny Malay state. On their final visit to this idyllic paradise the state's chieftain, Karain, has gone missing but during the night he swims out to the ship in a state of distress. The reader is now invited to make what he will of the story that follows.

Karain's distraught condition has been caused by the appearance of the ghost of his best friend, Pata Matara, whom he had killed some years earlier in a mission that went badly wrong. Matara's sister had violated cultural tradition by marrying a Dutch trader and Karain and Matara had vowed to track them both down and kill them. At the moment of revenge Karain had become so obsessed by the image of the girl that he killed his friend in order to save her. Pata Matara's ghost is now having its own revenge but by producing a Jubilee medallion bearing the image of Queen Victoria, one of the crew members persuades Karain that the ghost can be exorcized by the 'Great Queen, the most powerful thing the white men know' and Karain is able to return, now at peace with himself, to his people.

What is so unusual about 'Karain' is the way the reader is invited to participate in deciding between the cultural contrasts that are evoked in the story. Do we believe in 'the firm pulsating beat of the two ship's chronometers ticking off steadily the seconds of Greenwich Time' (p. 58) or in the 'carved images of devils with many arms and legs with snakes twined around their bodies, with twenty heads and holding a hundred swords' (p. 53)? Do we credit Queen Victoria with the same powers of exorcism as Karain's old sword-bearer who had previously protected his master from the ghost? Conrad expects us to have an opinion because, when Karain finally returns to his people, the narrator, in a uniquely direct appeal to the reader, asks 'I wonder what they thought; what he thought… what the reader thinks?' (p. 66)

However, it is in the final twist to the story, the final 'memory', that Conrad makes his real point. Years later, the skipper-narrator runs into an old crew member, Jackson, in London and they reminisce about Karain. As Jackson looks around him at the familiar scene he wonders which is real: the horses, the carriages and the policeman in a London street or the mystical events of the East brought back by the memory of that ghostly story of revenge:

> 'Yes, I see it, said Jackson slowly. It is there; it pants it runs it rolls; it is strong and alive; it would smash you if you didn't look out; but I'll be hanged if it is yet as real to me as… as the other thing… say, Karain's story. (p. 68)

'Amy Foster'

The bleak tale of 'Amy Foster', set in the English county of Kent, must have shocked the readers of the *Illustrated London News* in 1901 and Conrad's literary agent had some difficulty finding a magazine that would publish it (Stape, 1996: 31). It is Conrad's only story to feature a Pole living in England, so parallels have been drawn with his own experiences on arrival in his newly adopted country. Perhaps for this very reason, Conrad uses a double-narrator technique to distance the author even further from the story: an anonymous narrator tells us the story that his friend, a country doctor named Kennedy, has told him during a visit to his house in Kent.

A young Polish immigrant, Yanko Gooral, is the sole survivor when his ship bound for America is wrecked off the coast of Kent and he is literally washed up into the coastal village of Colebrook. Covered from head to foot in mud and filth he is spotted by a local farmer, and the sad story of mutual incomprehension begins: 'a sudden burst of rapid speech persuaded him at once that he had to do with an escaped lunatic' (Conrad, 1997: 105).

Gooral is locked up but the farmer's servant, Amy Foster, in an instinctive act of kindness, brings him half a loaf of bread. 'Through this act of impulsive pity he was brought back again within the pale of human relations with his new surroundings. He never forgot it – never' (p. 108). The scene is set for reconciliation, mutual understanding and cultural assimilation but none of it happens. To the astonishment of the village, Gooral marries Amy Foster and they have a son. Gooral wants his son to learn his language, be of his religion and understand his rhymes and dances, so his isolation from the rest of the village increases and he falls ill. In his delirium he shouts for a drink of water, but in Polish, and Amy, thinking she is being threatened, flees the house with her son. In the morning Gooral is found face down in a puddle of water and, despite Dr Kennedy's attention, he dies shortly afterwards.

The philosopher, Bertrand Russell, commented: 'I have wondered at times how much of (Yanko's) loneliness Conrad had felt among the English and had suppressed by a stern effort of will' (Conrad, 2002b: p. xviii).

The narrator

However, despite the powerful message of alienation, there is an element of optimism in 'Amy Foster', the personality of the inner narrator, Dr Kennedy. It cannot be by chance that Conrad chose to make him a former naval surgeon who had travelled widely, a biologist who had contributed papers to scientific societies:

> 'His intelligence is of a scientific order, of an investigating habit, and of that unappeasable curiosity which believes there is a particle of general truth in every mystery… He had the talent of making people talk to him freely and an inexhaustible patience in listening to their tales.' (Conrad, 1997: 95-6)

We can now recognize another role of the narrator in Conrad's stories namely to open up the possibility that things could be different. In 'An Outpost of Progress', we hear about events as they were, related by the omniscient author. The reader is required to take the story at face value: there is no alternative interpretation. But with a narrator, the situation is changed. In the first place, we are under no obligation to accept the narrator's perspective: his view does not carry the unique force of the writer's authority and our opinion is no less valid than his. Then the narrator, being outside the story, can take us outside of it, too, and suggest other ways of looking at it.

In 'Karain: A Memory' the skipper-narrator is regularly inviting us to look in and think again. When, for example, the sailor, Hollis, is looking for his Queen Victoria medallion, the narrator shares his feeling that:

> '… it seemed to me, during that moment of waiting, that the cabin of the schooner was becoming filled with a stir invisible and living as of subtle breaths. All the ghosts driven out of the unbelieving West by men who pretend to be wise and alone and at peace – all the homeless ghosts of an unbelieving world – appeared suddenly round the figure of Hollis bending over the box… ' (Conrad, 1997: 63)

The very words 'and it seemed to me' lead us straight to the question 'and how does it seem to you?' as we are invited to reflect on a White culture that is being described as unbelieving, deceitful and inhospitable. We are also being asked whether the British Queen-Empress is really much different in her perceived majesty and mystique to the exotic ruler of a far-off Malay state and we can begin to feel a cultural gap closing. The reader is being asked to match one set of cultural norms against another, the process culminating in the passage quoted earlier where one of the ship's crew, in the middle of a busy daytime London street, is more than half convinced that he believes in the existence of spirits. The narrator has persuaded us that another culture can offer a valid interpretation of the world even though we may never fully understand it.

In 'Amy Foster', Dr Kennedy offers the only ray of hope in the otherwise wholly dark and resentful environment of the village of Colebrook. Being a doctor, Kennedy is educated; being a scientist, Kennedy is rational; being a former naval officer and explorer, Kennedy has seen the world. It is Kennedy who pricks our consciences, deplores ignorant prejudice and regrets Gooral's death. Without the narrator it is hard to see how a different side of the story could ever have been imagined; with the narrator we are persuaded that prejudice *can* be overcome, strangers *can* be made welcome, foreigners *can* be understood, but only by an educated Dr Kennedy and not by an ignorant Farmer Smith.

Conclusion

Bertrand Russell wrote of Conrad:

> 'I felt, though I do not know whether he would have accepted such an image, that he thought of civilized and morally tolerable human life as a dangerous walk on a thin crust of barely cooled lava which at any moment might break and let the unwary sink into fiery depths.' (Baines, 1960: 448)

Eighty years after Conrad's death, those fiery depths are more apparent than ever and his writing offers no easy solutions to the international educator who is trying to strengthen that thin crust. Conrad was not an optimist and death, especially death by suicide, is prominent in his writing. But his uncompromising honesty, based on a breadth of experience of the world that measured even in terms of today's global mobility was exceptional, helps us to understand better the magnitude of our task.

On the one hand, Conrad was an ordinary man, with whom we can readily identify, who enjoyed the simple, if risky, life of the merchant navy. On the other hand he possessed a remarkable literary talent which he used to examine the thoughts and relationships of people living anything but simple lives, and often outside their cultural context.

A shared culture, in T.S. Eliot's description (1948), 'makes life worth living'. Conrad explores the behaviour of those who are cut off from a shared culture, those who have the imagination to glimpse the possibility of sharing a different culture and those who are rejected by a majority whose culture they cannot share. Each of these themes is explored against the background of a supreme White imperial culture whose values Conrad had the courage to call into question.

Reprinted by permission of Sage Publications Ltd from Journal of Research in International Education, Volume 3, No. 2
© Sage Publications & IBO, 2004

References

Baines, J. (1960) *Joseph Conrad. A Critical Biography.* London: Weidenfeld & Nicolson.

Bruner, J. S. (1996) *The Culture of Education.* Cambridge, MA: Harvard University Press.

Conrad, J. (1928) *Tales of Unrest.* New York: Doubleday & Doran.

Conrad, J. (1963) *The Nigger of the Narcissus, Typhoon and Other Stories.* London: Penguin Books.

Conrad, J. (1988) *A Personal Record.* Marlboro, VT: Marlboro.

Conrad, J. (1997) *Selected Short Stories.* Ware: Wordsworth Press

Conrad, J. (2002a) *Heart of Darkness and Other Tales.* Oxford: Oxford University Press

Conrad, J. (2002b) *Typhoon and Other Tales.* Oxford: Oxford University Press.

Eliot, T. S. (1948) *Notes Towards the Definition of Culture.* London: Faber & Faber.

Hayden, M. C. & Thompson, J. J. (1.995) International schools and international education: a relationship reviewed. *Oxford Review of Education* 21 (3). 327-45.

Hill, I. (2002) An International Baccalaureate perspective, in M. Hayden, J. J. Thompson and G. Walker (Eds) *International Education in Practice*, 28. London: Kogan Page.

IBE (1994) *Education Innovation and Information.* Geneva: International Bureau of Education.

IBO (1999) Subject Guide to Language A1. Geneva: IBO.

IBO (2002) Mission Statement. Geneva: IBO.

Knowles, O. & Moore, G. (Eds) (2001) *Oxford Reader's Companion to Conrad.* Oxford: Oxford University Press.

Langford, M. (1998) Global nomads, TCKs and international schools, in M. Hayden and J. Thompson (Eds) *International Education: Principles and Practice*, 28-43. London: Kogan Page.

Leavis, F. (1948) *The Great Tradition.* London: Chatto & Windus.

Peel, R. (1998) *Education for Life.* Geneva: IBO.

Stape, J. H. (Ed.) (1996) *Cambridge Companion to Joseph Conrad.* Cambridge: Cambridge University Press.

UNESCO (1974) *Recommendation Concerning Education for International Understanding.* Paris: UNESCO.

Walker, G. (2000) One-way streets of our culture, in *International Schools Journal* 19 (2). 11-19.

"At the heart of international education lies the appreciation of difference, in the sense both of valuing diversity and of calling into question previously unchallenged assumptions and prejudices."

Diversity and complexity are likely to be the two greatest challenges for the global citizen of the future and the following three articles are concerned with reconciling the diversity of human beings with the universality of the human condition.

'What does international education offer to a divided world?' argues that division can be a strength and examines how human beings relate to each other, to a group and to a sense of shared humanity. This lecture was given in memory of a teacher, Shane Walsh-Till, who was killed in the Bali bombing in 2002.

'Learning to live with others' takes its title from one of the four pillars of education proposed in the UNESCO publication known as the *Delors Report*. I propose, controversially, that teachers educating global citizens should unsettle traditions, welcome tensions and demand sacrifices.

'Our shared humanity: developing an international conscience' shifts the focus from our differences to the human qualities that we all have in common. The title is derived from the previous IB mission statement which urges the global citizen to be 'conscious of the shared humanity that binds all people together while respecting the variety of cultures and attitudes that make for the richness of life.'

What does international education offer to a divided world?

Introduction

I did not know Shane Walsh-Till, but shortly after his death Craig Boyce wrote me a spontaneous and very moving description of his colleague. I have also read Ann Poenisch's longer tribute in the ECIS publication, *is*: 'a wonderful role model for all teachers, young and old'. He was clearly a fine and much loved teacher and I hope I can pay appropriate tribute to his memory today by explaining why his work was so important and why those of us who continue it must never lose heart.

It is not easy to be positive at the moment with the United Kingdom, where I happen to be writing this, seriously disrupted by an Al-Qaeda security alert. The United Nations Security Council has just started a crucial debate in New York on the Iraqi weapons issue and even if that is resolved we have a queue of other crises, including the Arab-Israeli conflict and North Korea's nuclear programme, waiting in the wings.

I am reminded of Oscar Wilde's rather untypical words: 'It takes a great deal of courage to see the world in all its tainted glory, and still to love it' (Wilde, 1895). So let me start with two brief stories to help you to show that courage.

About six months ago I was in Berlin, perhaps with some of you, at the annual conference of the European Council of International Schools. I had not been in Berlin for 35 years and the city I remembered was physically divided in two by The Wall which was only a few years old and had become a powerful symbol of separation and oppression.

This time, I could not believe the transformation as I got out of the U-Bahn at Friedrichstrasse and walked to the Pergamon museum to see the archaeological remains from Babylon which used to be completely inaccessible in the Soviet sector of East Berlin. Today, Berlin is open and vibrant, symbolizing not only the unification of Germany but also of Europe. Things *can* get better; divisions *can* be healed.

In 1990, I went back to Cape Town where I had been a postgraduate student 25 years earlier. I stayed in my old hall of residence at the university and the morning after my arrival I happened to witness the annual student photograph being taken. I was amazed. At least half of the faces were coloured or black. In my own photograph, taken in the same spot 25 years earlier, every single student face is white. Things *can* get better; divisions *can* be healed. I am going to ask you to accept that as an act of faith.

The Guardian (2002) newspaper, often one of the United Kingdom's more morose broadsheets, summed up the events of 2002 as follows:

> 'The year 2002 was in many respects undoubtedly one of great trauma and travail; the coming year will doubtless not be much different. But look again at the bigger picture and it is possible to believe that slowly, uncertainly, and travelling by many strange roads, humanity is coming to know itself; that to know is to begin to care; and that by caring, every one of us can make a difference.'

Division and diversity

What difference can you and I make? To remind you of the title of this lecture, *what does international education*, which is our business, *offer to a divided world?*

My answer, to which I shall continue to return, is that international education can help young people understand the divided world better. We have to be honest and realistic so let me substitute, just for a moment, the words International Baccalaureate Organization for 'international education', which is not unreasonable since the IBO is a major player in the real world of international education.

The IBO is not an aid agency; it has no experience of the reality of peace-keeping; it has never worked with refugees; it is not a political forum. The IBO is concerned from first to last with the process of education and, to adapt the famous introduction to the charter of UNESCO, if it is *in the minds of men* that the divisions occur, it will be in those same *minds of men* that they will be addressed – through education. That is another act of faith to which you must hold today: the potential power of education to bring about change.

But let me now turn your expectations of this lecture upside down by insisting that we should count ourselves very fortunate indeed that the world *is* a divided place because if it were not, life would be unimaginably dull: a world populated by the human equivalents of Dolly the cloned sheep. This deadening prospect is nowhere better described than by

George Orwell (1949) in his novel *1984*: the same clothes, the same food, the same thoughts, the same soul-destroying uniformity and conformity. Winston Smith, the novel's hero, writes in his clandestine diary:

> 'To the future or to the past, to a time when thought is free, when men are different from one another and do not live alone – to a time when truth exists and what is done cannot be undone.

> From the age of uniformity, from the age of solitude, from the age of Big Brother, from the age of doublethink – greetings!'

Division is a necessary precursor of diversity. Only by being divided from each other do we assume our own unique individuality. We identify ourselves through our differences and we remain deeply suspicious of the process of genetic cloning. Our own children, though closely similar in genetic composition, are not only given different names; they are quickly encouraged to assume different personalities.

The individual, the group and human kind

But we are clearly not the human equivalent of unconnected gas molecules each in isolated motion, oblivious of the others until we collide with them. As we look down from an upstairs window on a crowd of youngsters milling about in a playground, we soon realize that the movement is not that of random individuality. Groups begin to coalesce, bringing together those who have something in common: a game to enjoy, a lunch to share, a secret to protect and a common language with which to do it.

There is both safety and stimulus within a group and so cultures begin to form, bound together by a common language, common traditions and common values. Human minds are not programmed on an individual basis but, to use the powerful metaphor of Hofstede· by the group's culture, the 'software of the mind' (Hofstede, 1991).

As we look across the world we observe how few of these cultures have been neatly enclosed within geographically defined nation states. Japan is – or was – one of the rare examples. Most of them do not fit the boundaries and the messy business of trying to shoehorn ethnic majorities and minorities into particular parts of the globe accounted for most of the blood shed in conflicts throughout the 20th century.

However, while politicians and their armies have been trying to assign people to places, many aspects of ordinary lives – health, shopping and environmental quality as well as sport, entertainment and fashion – have refused to be so tightly constrained; they roam internationally across the globe.

Let me then describe the 'divided world' of the 21st century:

- we are individual human beings, spending much of the day in the company of our own thoughts, worries and aspirations. '*On mourra seul*,' wrote the 17th century French scientist, Blaise Pascal (1660);

- then we are part of a group, a larger culture held together by shared values, with its roots in our families, which controls our responses to the most important questions in our lives. 'A shared culture,' wrote the poet T S Eliot (1948), 'is what makes life worth living';

- finally, we are part of the human species which has its own struggle for economic, political and environmental survival. '... but what thrilled you,' says Marlow, describing the native Africans in Conrad's novel (1902) *Heart of Darkness*, 'was just the thought of their humanity – like yours...' In the end, we all come from the same origins.

If this is a fair description of the divided world, then the role of international education, I want to argue, is not to try to heal it, but to help our students to understand it and to live with all its ambiguities.

- How do human beings relate to *each other*;

- how do they relate to *a culture;* and

- how do they relate to their *shared humanity*?

It is making sense of these relationships, the personal, the cultural and the universal, that is the challenge to international education.

In the few minutes that remain, I can do no more than scratch the surface of a topic that is preoccupying the community of international educators. I deliberately choose the term 'educators' because it includes teachers, administrators and researchers and, for me, one of the most stimulating features of international education is the large number of practitioners who are not only practising, but also researching and writing about what they are preaching. I doubt if there is any other area of education at the moment where the traditional barriers between theory and practice have been so effectively broken down.

Knowing ourselves and others

Let me start, then, with a brief look at that first level at which we are divided, the interactions of individuals, by recommending an article that appears in the second number of the new *Journal of Research in International Education*. Patrick Sherlock (2002), from the Nova Scotia Community College in Canada, has written about emotional intelligence in the international curriculum, drawing in particular on the work of Daniel Goleman:

> 'Emotional intelligence begins with self-awareness and self-understanding, progressing towards the goal of the student learning to manage his or her own emotions. They then learn to become sensitive to the emotions of others, improving their communication skills, developing empathy and employing active listening skills. The resulting awareness, respect and understanding, I would argue, underpin international education.'

Two features of this article particularly attracted my attention. First, its reference to what is fast becoming a 'sacred text' for international educators, namely the so-called *Delors Report*, 'Learning: The Treasure Within', the report to UNESCO of the International Commission on Education for the Twenty-first Century.

This is the report that speaks of learning to know, learning to do, learning to live with others and learning to be. A single sentence from Jacques Delors' introduction encapsulates my lecture today: '... people need gradually to become world citizens without losing their roots and while continuing to play an active part in the life of their nation and their local community' (UNESCO, 1996)

Second, Sherlock refers to a device, a model, that I had not met before, that helps us to understand aspects of interpersonal communication, to see ourselves as others see us, the so-called Johari Window. Four panes of glass describe the self: public, private, blind and unknown. In each case the glass separates me from others; our communication must pass through it.

- The *public self* represents my free and open exchange of information with others; the glass is clear and two-way.

- The *private self* is that part of me part that, for whatever reasons – positive and negative – I choose not to share with others and my learning may thereby remain blocked. I need to understand that cultural difference will be a powerful motivator in protecting a private self.

- The *blind self* is what others see in me but I cannot see in myself. Clearly it is crucial to cultural empathy and my insensitivity towards my own behaviour, which will be reinforced in a cultural majority's insensitivity towards a cultural minority, can be shocking when it is exposed.

- The *unknown self* is that part of me that neither I nor others know; it is buried in the unconscious and particular learning situations (drama comes to mind) must be devised to encourage it into the open.

The four windows are interrelated and their relative sizes can change. A curriculum that sets out to develop emotional intelligence, argues Sherlock, can use this model to encourage greater awareness of myself and thus, since the windows link me to you, a greater awareness of those around me. I found this helpful because it will enable me to think more about myself, about the other person and about the differences that divide us. I encourage you to read it.

Understanding culture

Let me now turn to people in groups. I read somewhere recently that a fish does not understand the concept of water until it is taken out of it and that must be true of the human's understanding of culture. In that sense the third culture kids, removed from their culture, could have something important to tell us. But I have my doubts because in most cases they have never really 'belonged' and therefore do not understand what they are missing.

So, although *Newsweek* (2003) has recently discovered them and has made much of their special qualities ("Sure, it's a weird life sometimes, but it's just the way we are. I wouldn't trade it for the world," says an example), I do not see the future belonging to the global nomads but rather to those whose minds are running on the software of their cultures, and that includes most of us here today.

Describing culture, its constituent parts, its development over time and its influence on behaviour is surely one of the most important challenges to the international educator. There are many different approaches of which a study of world literature can be particularly stimulating. Just three novels – André Makine's *Le Testament Français*, David Guterson's *Snow Falling On Cedars* and Orhan Pamuk's *My Name Is Red* – can take the reader into worlds where rational people cannot help thinking and acting the way they do.

Then there are the many different forms of simulation and role-play which require students to respond to an unfamiliar cultural context. The most sophisticated are the model United Nations of which there are now dozens of examples around the world.

I believe these are powerful learning tools for international education because students are required to research the background to an important issue, ask how that particular country would react, make a persuasive case and then try to negotiate an agreement and, in the one I am most familiar with, students are not allowed to represent their own country. This particular example, at the International School of Geneva, was launched in 1953 by an inspirational history teacher, Robert Leach, and the IBO will be proud to join with Ecolint to celebrate its 50th anniversary in December.

A different angle on cultural difference is described in the growing volume of research evidence in the field of social psychology. I wish I had been more familiar with the work of Hofstede (1991), Trompenaars and Hampden-Turner (1997) when I was director general of the International School of Geneva because I would have been better prepared for some of the reactions of teachers, parents and governors that a number of my proposals provoked.

Just to give one example: I come from a culture which is prepared to suspend judgement in order to move a project to the next step, to maintain momentum. This involves significant risk and many of my Francophone colleagues would object to what they perceived as an irresponsible 'let's give it a try' approach. At the time their reaction seemed to be deliberately obstructive; I now realise that it had much deeper cultural origins.

Who was right, I or they, and can some cultures be more right than others? The answer must be 'yes' but only in the context of the question, 'more right for what?' Are we seeking conciliation or competition? Do we accept risk or insist upon security? Do we bow to authority or encourage dissent? Do we tolerate corruption or demand probity? These issues are addressed by Professor Zhou Nanzhao, a member of the Delors Commission and currently a member of the IBO's Council of Foundation. In a stimulating personal contribution to the *Delors Report,* he discusses the positive and negative features of Asian cultural traditions, not in the abstract, but in the context of educational and economic development (Nanzhao, 1996). He notes for example, the negative gender bias which still results in a disproportionate school drop-out rate for girls in the Asian region and the positive effect that the widespread respect for education has on progress in the region. Again, I encourage you to read it.

Seeking universal values

You will have realized that I am moving from the particular to the more general: from individual diversity, to cultural diversity to the 'holy grail' of international educators, a set of universal values that transcends cultural difference and applies to everyone. Surely we can set aside our cultural differences in the face of the bigger challenge of living together on a rather small and vulnerable planet. Can we not all sign up to a code of universally acceptable behaviour?

At a fundamental level there do indeed seem to be some widely shared values, or at least preferences: honesty, freedom and justice, for example. In practice, however, there are many different cultural variants of 'being honest' and many cultures would not hesitate to put loyalty above honesty. As I have pointed out elsewhere (Walker, 1999) many governments protest their concern for 'human rights' but in practice attach a value to it that puts it low down their list of daily priorities.

Although every nation has signed up to the United Nations' Universal Declaration of Human Rights, not one of them abides strictly by the terms of all its articles and some would argue that the Universal Declaration tries to enshrine concepts that have been rejected as Western-oriented 'human rights imperialism' by some non-Western cultures. However, given the overwhelmingly superior economic and military position of the West, they are in no position – for the time being – to argue.

The United States stands accused of manipulating the United Nations for its own interests. But do we really believe that the current opposition within the Security Council – for example, France, Germany, Russia and China – are acting from anything other than national self-interest? The lack of progress in reforming the Security Council itself, which still reflects the state of the world in 1945, indicates the profound reluctance of nations to subordinate their particular interests to the more general needs of the world.

So: is the search for workable universal human values a hopeless one? Harvard Professor, Samuel Huntington, believes so, arguing that the future great divisions among humankind will be cultural rather than ideological or economic as in the past:

'The world will be shaped in large measure by the interactions among seven or eight major civilizations. These include Western, Confucian, Japanese, Islamic, Hindu, Slavic-Orthodox, Latin American and possibly African civilizations… Civilizations are differentiated from each other by history, culture, tradition and, most important, religion. The people of different civilizations have different views on the relations between God and man, the individual and the group, the citizen and the state, parents and children, husband and wife, as well as differing views on the relative importance of rights and responsibilities, liberty and authority, equality and hierarchy' (Huntington, 1993).

'The very notion,' argues Huntington, 'that there could be a "universal civilization" is a very Western idea, directly at odds with the particularism of most Asian societies and their emphasis on what distinguishes one people from another.'

A different view is taken by those working in the Division of Philosophy and Ethics at UNESCO. Looking at the values and ethics gathered from five sources: intergovernmental documents, international commissions and conferences, non-governmental projects and surveys, individuals and different religious traditions, four basic sections have been identified around which to organize ethical values and principles:

- Relationship to nature

- Human fulfilment

- Individual and community

- Justice.

Within each section, no attempt has been made to conceal areas of potential conflict. Under Justice, for example, we read, 'We must live simply in order that others may simply live' and under Relationship to nature, 'Continuation of economic development at the present rate endangers the rights of future generations to life and a healthy environment' (Kim, 1999)

The scope of our ethical practice, argues UNESCO, can no longer stop at the edge of our family, our society, or our nation. Hope lies in action in accordance with shared ethics.

However risky, I believe the search for universally-shared values is essential and to explain why, I am going to end this lecture by returning to Berlin. But before that, let me try to sum up what I have been trying to say:

1.   I believe that humanity is divided in many different ways which create its essential diversity.

2.   Attempts to remove the divisions often consist of one group imposing its culture upon another in the name of 'universal values'.

3.   Instead, I believe the challenge is to recognize, to understand and to tolerate diversity. In the words of Richard Pearce, in an article to be published later this year, 'How can we respect authentic distinction but not practise hostility?' (Pearce, 2003).

4.   This means first understanding oneself and one's relationship to other individuals. I have suggested one particular device that may help this process.

5.   Then it means understanding culture and its importance in determining group behaviour. I have proposed a number of different approaches to this challenge.

6.   Finally, I have presented two opposing views on the feasibility of agreeing universal values upon which human kind can agree and build a more peaceful world.

Back to Berlin

I have already described my exhilaration travelling in complete freedom around Berlin, so it was with a sense of shock that I read the name of the terminus to which my train was heading in the south-western suburbs of the city: Wannsee. On 20 January 1942, a group of 15 senior Nazi officials gathered in a villa on the shores of the lake to write the Wannsee Protocol describing the Final Solution through extermination of the Jewish people in Europe. The group was led by Reinhard Heydrich who was 39 and a talented violinist. Of the remaining 14, ten had university degrees and eight had doctorates; their average age was under 40.

Historians now believe that the Wannsee Protocol did not establish a new policy; it merely made official the existing widespread practice (Roseman, 2003). Already, in Poland, Czechoslovakia, Rumania, Hungary and Russia, tens of thousands of people who were different – because they were Jews, gypsies, physically handicapped, homosexual – were being murdered indiscriminately by Germans at all levels in the hierarchy, from the Nazi officials at the top to the ordinary soldiers at the bottom. It was against an existing culture of mass murder that a policy of genocide was written down at Wannsee.

I want to draw two conclusions from this low mark in history with which to bring my lecture to a close. First, the holocaust was a deliberate attempt to remove difference and impose greater uniformity; to make the world, if you like, a neater, better organized and more coherent place. Europe would be less divided. Second, it was made possible because a group of powerful people decided, and others, who might have stopped them failed to do so, decided that humanity had no meaning; that there were no common values that encompassed every single human being.

I believe it is the challenge of reconciling the diversity of human beings with the universality of the human condition that lies at the heart of international education. Shane Walsh-Till was part of a growing community of international educators who have devoted their professional lives to this challenge. If they have one thing in common, it is their ability to live with ambiguity and compromise because there is no simple solution. But, thanks to them, our understanding is increasing and I have deliberately quoted from the growing body of knowledge in this lecture.

I want to end with two contrasting statements which I hope capture the essence of my lecture. The first is by the Australian poet, Mary Gilmore, entitled 'Nationality' (1942):

'I have grown past hate and bitterness,
I see the world as one;
But though I can no longer hate,
My son is still my son.

'All men at God's round table sit,
And all men must be fed;
But this loaf in my hand,
This loaf is my son's bread.'

The second is from the 13th century Persian writer, Jelaluddin Rumi:

'Out beyond ideas of wrong-doing and right-doing, there is a field. I will meet you there. When the soul lies down in that grass, the world is too full to talk about. Ideas, language, even the phrase "each other" does not make any sense. I will meet you there.'

Chinese International School, Hong Kong:
Shane Walsh-Till Memorial Lecture, March 2003

References

Conrad, J. (1902) *Heart of Darkness*. Penguin, 1973, p51.

Eliot, T. S. (1948) *Notes Towards the Definition of Culture*. London: Faber & Faber.

Gilmore, M. (1942) Nationality. *Selected Poems*. ETT Imprint, Sydney, 2004. Reprinted by kind permission of ETT Imprint.

Hofstede, G. (1991) *Cultures and Organizations*. London: Harper Collins Business.

Huntington, S. P. (1993) The Clash of Civilizations. Original article from *Foreign Affairs Summer* 1993 vol 72 No3 (or the book of the same title, Free Press 2002 paperback).

Kim, Y. (1999) *A common framework for the ethics of the 21st century*. UNESCO.

Nanzhao, Zhou. (1996) in *Delors Report*. *Ibid* p239.

Newsweek, 27 January 2003.

Orwell, G. (1949) *1984*. Penguin, 1954, p26.

Pascal, B. (1660) *Pensées*.

Pearce, R. (2003) Cultural values for international schools. *International Schools Journal*. Vol XXII No 2, April 2003, pp59-65.

Roseman, M. (2003) *The Villa, the Lake, the Meeting*. London: Penguin.

Sherlock, P. (2002) Emotional intelligence in the international curriculum. *Journal of Research in International Education*. Vol 1 No 2.

The Guardian leading article, 23 December 2002.

Trompenaars, F. & Hampden-Turner, C. M. (1997) *Riding the Waves of Culture*. London: Nicholas Brealey Publishing Ltd.

UNESCO (1996) Learning: The Treasure Within. *Delors Report*, p17.

Walker, G. (1999) Our shared values: "Where does Altas stand?" *To Educate the Nations 2* (see also p91 of this book).

Wilde, O. (1895) *An Ideal Husband*.

Learning to live with others

Introduction

Your conference title 'How do we promote the international dimension in national schools?' is not only appropriate for this region but, as I hope you realize, is absolutely mainstream for the organization as a whole. Let me explain why; but first I must tell you a little about my own background in education.

I am very much a state school person. I was educated at a state primary school and then at a state grammar school. A state grant enabled me to attend university and it was no surprise when I started my career teaching science in a state school. Later on I became deputy head of a state comprehensive school and then head of two state comprehensive schools. In the 1980s I helped to found the Centre for the Study of Comprehensive Schools which was committed to improving standards in state schools in the United Kingdom. My writing during this period was often strongly critical of independent schools and of the disproportionate influence that they exerted within the society of my own country.

My conversion, if that is the right word, came in 1990. Exactly 25 years after I had been a graduate student at the University of Cape Town, I was given the opportunity to return to South Africa to write for Times Newspapers. As I started to gather information about black and white education during this extraordinary period of political change, I came to realize that the South African independent schools, many of them international both in composition and in spirit, had played a significant part in the battle against apartheid. They had maintained, sometimes in difficult and dangerous circumstances, a small but independent window from which to look out at the rest of the world of education. Within weeks of returning to Britain, I saw the advertisement for the post of director general of the International School of Geneva and the rest, as they say, is history.

More recently, in the autumn of 1999, some historic decisions were reached within the International Baccalaureate Organization. I had just taken up my post as Director General and the executive committee of the Council of Foundation organized a weekend retreat at Pennyhill Park, close to London. It had become clear that two broad options were open to the organization: to maintain the existing rate of expansion of authorized schools or to seek new ways of widening the influence of the IB's three programmes of international education. In the event, we decided to do both! Our present annual rate of increase of schools is well over 10%, which is impressive, but it means that in a decade's time there will still be only about 2500, a drop in the ocean of the world's total of schools. So the Council has agreed to develop other ways of extending the IB's influence and this, to my satisfaction, is to include collaborating with state systems of education, because it is obviously there that the major influence for the future lies.

Defining an international dimension

So: you could not have chosen a more relevant theme – how do we promote the international dimension in national schools? – and I hope that I shall be able to make a useful contribution to your thinking during the next few minutes. But I shall not get very far without some suggestion of what we mean by the phrase *an international dimension.*

- I hope we mean more than a change of name. I am amazed at the way the British School of Ruritania is transformed overnight into the International School of Ruritania in order to attract a more cosmopolitan group of parents

- I hope we mean something more substantial than the famous 'five Fs of international education': food, festivals, famous people, fashion and flags

- I hope, dare I say it, that we mean even more than becoming an IB school, though that may well be an important step in the right direction.

For me the key element of an international dimension is providing an education from which young people can learn to live together. One of the main reasons behind the creation in 1924 of the world's oldest international school in Geneva was to encourage young people of different nationalities to live together in the spirit of the newly created League of Nations. The main goal of the United World Colleges is, to quote their mission statement, to 'encourage young people to become responsible citizens, politically and environmentally aware, committed to the ideals of peace, justice, understanding and cooperation…' and I doubt if there is an international school in the world without a similar statement in its brochure. Indeed, research has confirmed that for students and for teachers in international schools the highest priority is the opportunity for students of different nationalities to mix together.

But, you might ask, what is uniquely *international* about learning to live together? And the answer of course is nothing; learning to live together has always been one of the main socialising aims of attending school. But as the world shrinks and many so-called *national* schools welcome students from as many different cultures as so-called *international* schools, the challenge has assumed a new dimension. Perhaps those who work in international education have some advice to give to those who work in national education who want to address more effectively their growing global responsibilities because we can no longer be satisfied with national responses to challenges that have to be viewed in an international perspective.

However, let us not for one moment suppose that international schools have all the answers. I have seen how students in international schools readily polarise into national groupings outside the classroom. I have read recently about thinly disguised racism in a number of international schools in Africa. I shared with some of you, at the regional conference in Oman, the depressing reversion to the nationalist stereotype of Serbian alumni of the International School of Geneva during the NATO bombing of Belgrade (see page 93). And I recently listened to the concern of the heads of the United World Colleges at their apparent inability to shift Arab-Israeli antagonism amongst their students. We are all trying to roll a very heavy boulder up a very steep hill.

A UNESCO initiative

In 1993, UNESCO, the United Nations Education, Scientific and Cultural Organization, with which the IBO has official consultancy status, created an International Commission on Education for the Twenty-First Century to produce a report that would shape educational thinking in the new millennium. Published in 1996, the report was entitled *Learning: the Treasure Within* or, more commonly, the *Delors Report* after its chairman, Jacques Delors. My own copy was given to me by one of the 15 members of the commission, the distinguished Chinese professor, Zhou Nanzhao, who is now a member of the IBO's Council of Foundation.

The *Delors Report* identified four essential pillars of education:

- learning to know
- learning to do

- learning to live together

- learning to be.

Last week, UNESCO chose the theme of learning to live together *(l'éducation pour tous pour apprendre à vivre ensemble)* for its 46th International Conference on Education which brought government representatives from more than 100 nations to Geneva. We can therefore say with complete confidence that this particular topic is at the top of the agenda of debates about the future of education in most parts of the world.

Working at a difficult problem

How can we best develop an education for learning to live together? I think we must start by accepting that living together is not easy, should not be taken for granted, is not something that comes naturally. Whether we look at the most intimate, personal human level where we note that one in three marriages in Denmark (two in three in Sweden) end in divorce or whether we look at the political, global level where we note that no fewer than 150 armed conflicts took place during the decade of the 1990s, we realise that living together does not happen spontaneously. In thermodynamic terms (and now I speak as a science teacher) that means that if it is going to happen at all, we have to put some work into it.

I therefore start from a very pragmatic *point de départ*, that of enlightened self-interest. People come together, learn to live together and make the necessary sacrifices to stay together when they believe it is in their interest to do so. This is what lay behind Rousseau's Social Contract published in 1762; it lay behind Immanuel Kant's proposal for a league of nations made in 1795 and today it lies behind, uneasily I agree, the United Nations itself, founded in 1945. So, let us accept that learning to live together does not come naturally, but requires a lot of thought, understanding and hard work. It is a matter of the head rather than the heart.

The UNESCO conference to which I have just referred was presented with a key discussion document which identified seven basic educational requirements for learning to live together:

1.   acquiring the capacity to deal with rapid change in all walks of life

2.   becoming active citizens, participating in political life in its widest sense

3. defending and promoting human rights

4. reconciling the local community with the wider world

5. learning languages

6. knowing how to assess the impact on daily life of scientific developments

7. being able to use new technologies of communication.

It is impossible to quarrel with such a list. But it is also hard to know what to do about it, each component being enormous in its scope and implications – for the curriculum, for the teachers and for the provision of resources. Perhaps it is responding to that kind of multiple challenge that turns ordinary people into government ministers, but I need something more focused and for the rest of this talk I am going to ask how *teachers* can help educate young people in learning to live together.

Since almost everyone in this room either is, or has been, a teacher, I hesitate to point out the obvious: that the success of every educational endeavour depends upon a teacher. The teachers may be 'online' or they may be 'distant' but someone, somewhere, is presenting material in a manner that encourages or discourages students to learn. School buildings are important, the number of books in the library matters, the IB programmes are the gateway to an enlightened education, but without the right teachers the whole lot comes crashing down.

I am now going to argue, provocatively I hope, that the promotion of an international dimension in national schools needs teachers:

●   who unsettle traditions

●   who welcome tensions

●   who demand sacrifices

because I believe each of these is necessary if we are to learn to live together better. Teaching, as the title of the 1960s book by Postman and Weingartner told us, is a subversive activity. Socrates paid for his subversion of the youth of Athens with his life and to help present my case I am going to introduce someone just as subversive, who had a huge admiration for Socrates, but lived a little nearer to our times: Michel de Montaigne.

Montaigne (as he is generally known) was born in 1533 and died, at exactly my age, in 1592. He lived in Gascony, though he travelled widely, and in 1571 he inherited his father's lands and title and retired to Montaigne to write his masterpiece, three sets of *Essays*. I am convinced that Montaigne would have approved of the IB programmes but we would have had a problem accommodating him as a diploma candidate: his first language was Latin and, as far as I know, we do not offer that as Language A1!

There are many reasons for taking Montaigne seriously, even four centuries after his death. Here are just a few:

- he is open-minded, modest and never takes himself too seriously

- in addition to his own travel experience, he read widely about the travels of others, especially to the New World (remember Columbus had set sail some 40 years before Montaigne's birth)

- his life was disrupted by the Wars of Religion, fought on and off for nearly 40 years; living in France at that time must have been rather like living in the Balkans today

- his knowledge of the classical writers was prodigious, though sometimes inaccurate; Montaigne honestly admits that few of his ideas are wholly original

- the Essays make wonderful reading with something for everyone: on friendship, education, prayer, prognostication, cruelty, old age and so on; over 100 in all

- they are very accessible, translated into every major language.

Teachers unsettle traditions

One essay in particular is relevant to my first theme: the unsettling of traditions. It is called: 'On habit: and on never easily changing a traditional law.' You will remember that the first of the seven UNESCO requirements for an education for learning to live together was the capacity to deal with rapid change. It has always been assumed that strong roots in our familiar past give us the necessary anchorage for our confidence in facing an unfamiliar future. I am beginning to wonder if there is any relationship between the two. Listen to Montaigne:

'For in truth, Habit is a violent and treacherous schoolteacher. Gradually and stealthily she slides her authoritative foot into us...

'Our judgement's power to see things is lulled to sleep once we grow accustomed to anything.

'But the principal activity of custom is so to seize us and to grip us in her claws that it is hardly in our power to struggle free and to come back into ourselves, where we can reason and argue about her ordinances.'

Here, I suggest, is the greatest challenge to learning to live together – the assumption that *life has always been like this and we do not want it to change:*

- The nation's coinage has always had the monarch's head on it
- Such-and-such a religious sect has always had the right to march through this area
- We have always had a public holiday to celebrate victory in that battle
- Those people will never surrender their historic right to carry firearms
- We always sing that triumphalist song at the end of our ceremony

and so on…

A good teacher will challenge these habits by insisting that students think about them rationally. But have you noticed how *habit* has already become *custom*? And over the page, *custom* becomes *tradition* and before the end of the essay, Montaigne is writing about *culture*. Are we then beginning to deny our students their very birthright, their culture?

Recently a first novel, *White Teeth*, by Zadie Smith, won critical acclaim in Britain and America. It describes how two generations of families from three different cultures learn to live together in London. Samad came to Britain after the Second World War and he is desperate to ensure that his twin sons, born in London, retain their Bangladeshi roots. I wonder if you agree with this extract:

'If religion is the opium of the people, tradition is an even more sinister analgesic, simply because it rarely appears sinister. If religion is a tight band, a throbbing vein and a needle, tradition is a far homelier concoction: poppy seeds ground into tea, a sweet cocoa drink laced with cocaine; the kind of thing your grandmother might have made. To Samad… tradition was culture and culture led to roots, these were good, these were untainted principles… You could get nowhere by telling him that weeds, too, have tubers, or that the first sign of loose teeth is something rotten, something degenerate, deep within the gums.'

White Teeth, Zadie Smith, (Hamish Hamilton, 2000)

I can still remember the moment (not unlike 'where were you when President Kennedy was shot?') when the headmaster of my secondary school gently suggested that all that pink colouring that marked out the British Empire on our rather old atlases might not be a matter for such pride after all. I was stunned and at that moment he opened up a small but significant gap between me and my parents. But that is precisely what subversion involves.

Teachers welcome tensions

One of the problems of school is that students expect answers. They expect simple, truthful answers that can be backed up with evidence, usually in a form to quote in examinations. Teachers are expected to resolve uncertainties, remove ambiguities and cut Gordian Knots. The idea that the electron might be a particle, but then again might be an electromagnetic wave; the possibility that the First World War might or might not have been precipitated by an assassination in Sarajevo – these are about the limits of the suspension of a youthful need-to-know.

Montaigne was a sceptic. He was fascinated by philosophy; but he was just as fascinated by the weaknesses (especially the physical weaknesses) of ordinary human beings. His essays attempt a reconciliation of the two against a background of religious and social turbulence. In one of them he reflects on the experience of being knocked senseless from his horse during a skirmish and the way it affected his fear of dying.

Education for learning to live together must lead students to the knowledge that there are no simple answers to the most important contemporary questions and that tensions between conflicting points of view have to be lived with, argued about and frequently left unresolved. There are no sunlit uplands of peaceful certainty to strive towards. The Delors Report, which I mentioned earlier, contains a section entitled 'Tensions to be overcome'. They are as follows:

- global versus local
- universal versus individual

- tradition versus modernity
- long-term versus short-term considerations
- competition versus equality of opportunity
- expansion of knowledge versus the human capacity to assimilate it
- spiritual versus material.

I cannot conceive how these tensions are ever to be 'overcome' since they mark out the boundaries of human activity. We learn to live together within these boundaries by recognizing that different cultures at different periods of history will adopt different responses to these major tensions. Moreover, to those who have the courage to look beyond simple solutions, the tensions themselves can produce new and creative responses.

I must acknowledge, however, that in one fundamental way, Montaigne was able to resolve his doubts without recourse to philosophy – through his religious belief. Throughout the Wars of Religion he maintained his deep Catholic faith, but this did not prevent him keeping an open, undefended house for all parties to visit. In his essays he makes no attempt to reconcile the philosophical with the religious; for him they are two different issues. For those who have lost their faith, 400 years later, religion can offer:

> '… neither joy, nor love, nor light
> nor certitude, nor peace, nor help for pain'

The tensions remain unresolved and we must therefore educate our students to live with them and to use them.

Teachers demand sacrifices

I mentioned earlier a recent meeting I had with the heads of all the United World Colleges. At one point our host, David Sutcliffe, retiring head of the UWC Adriatic, made the unfashionable comment: "The United World Colleges are nothing without a sense of sacrifice". It provoked little reaction, but it has remained with me ever since.

It is an obvious observation that living together demands an element of sacrifice, of giving up something that you value. Even the powerfully primitive biological bonding that comes with children is sometimes not enough to balance the huge sacrifice that is demanded from the parents. I have been told, by my mother amongst others, that during the Second

World War the most unlikely people formed supportive friendships that were only conceivable in the context of a shared threat. It was a time when the word *neighbour* meant more than an Australian soap. To use a very English expression, it was a time when people were prepared to muck in together.

Today, when some of us have so many material benefits, so much independence and so many different choices in front of us, the concept of sacrifice often seems very distant indeed. But returning to my theme of enlightened self-interest, for how much longer can we ignore the scenes of battle in Seattle, Prague, Davos and Genoa?

On this issue, Montaigne misses a trick because he seems to be unaware of one of the most remarkable passages in classical literature, a tiny fragment that has remained from the writings of Democritus, best known as the originator of the atomic theory. Democritus wrote the following:

> 'When the powerful in a state, face to face with the weak, are prepared to make financial sacrifices for them and to help them and to satisfy them, that is the time when you get, first, compassion and then the end of isolation and the appearance of comradeship and mutual defence, and then civic agreement and then other benefits beyond the capacity of anyone to enumerate in full.'

In other words, harmony and unity can only be the result of a deliberate decision by the haves to share their good fortune with the have-nots; to make a deliberate sacrifice. It is important to note that Democritus was almost certainly inspired by an actual event when a chief magistrate celebrated his election by releasing large numbers of people from the burden of slavery.

There are many ways in which IB teachers can encourage their students to – let me bypass the word sacrifice and use instead – muck in together. Creativity, Action, Service is an obvious example, but there will be 101 different opportunities for young people to get used to giving something up in order to learn to live together more harmoniously with other people. It might even be one of those dubious habits we were talking about earlier.

Perhaps the biggest sacrifice for many people, especially articulate people, is to give up their language, their mother tongue, and I am conscious that nearly every one of you present today is listening in at least your second language, for which I am truly grateful. Why does the IBO put such an emphasis on learning a foreign language? Simple communication is one good reason. Cultural understanding for me is less convincing because I have never met more than a handful of people who were genuinely bi-cultural. But perhaps the best reason is to make a sacrifice: to admit to someone that if I am going to learn to live with you then I must put myself at a distinct psychological disadvantage by speaking your language.

Summary

It is time to sum up and, I hope, to remind you of some themes that you may want to take forward into your discussions. In the last few minutes, I have:

- complimented you on your choice of theme for the conference because I believe it has become central to the IBO's future

- made a personal interpretation of that theme by saying that, for me, the distinctive feature about an international dimension in education is learning to live together.

I have then insisted that our teachers play the key role in this process and, with the help of the 16th century French philosopher, Montaigne, I have identified three challenges which I hope will be sufficiently controversial to keep you arguing for the rest of the conference:

- unsettling traditions
- welcoming tensions
- demanding sacrifices.

A story

Let me end, in the words of Montaigne, *'dérobons ici la place d'un conte'* – let us steal a little room here for a story.

Back in May, I addressed the senior students' farewell dinner at a very large IB public high school in Florida. I had decided to start in a light-hearted way by quoting the description of Florida from a gazetteer that was published in 1782. But as I came to think about it, I realised that it was not light-hearted at all and instead I based my whole speech on the quotation. Here is the passage in question:

'Here are a great number of native Americans, who are of a red copper colour; with long coarse black hair, and without beards, and have no hair on their bodies. They go almost naked, smear their bodies with oil, and worship the sun. They bring their children up to warlike exercises, hunting and swimming. Both men and women are exceedingly active, and they can climb up the highest trees with incredible agility. They have no European animals but what are brought from the settlements; nor are the birds, trees, or plants like those with us.'

The passage is insidious in the way it biases the reader against those native Americans. The author does this using a number of simple techniques that show us how *not* to learn to live with others:

• he emphasises the differences between us and them

• he implies they and their environment are less interesting than we and ours

• he makes a deliberate choice of skills that we do not value (climbing trees)

• he sows seeds of suspicion and fear

• he cannot resist drawing attention to different religious beliefs.

In complete contrast, Montaigne writes in one of his essays about the Brazilian indians (the first Europeans had landed in Brazil in 1557):

'… they inhabit a land with a most delightful countryside and a temperate climate, so that, from what I have been told by my sources, it is rare to find anyone ill there. I have been assured that they never saw a single man bent with age, toothless, blear-eyed or tottering. They dwell along the sea shore, shut in to landwards by great lofty mountains, on a stretch of land some hundred leagues in width. They have fish and flesh in abundance which bear no resemblance to ours; these they eat simply cooked.'

This description comes from a completely different mindset which respects, wonders about, explores and takes delight in the new, the unexpected and the different.

The essay is called 'On the cannibals' and towards the end Montaigne is forced to confront the classic dilemma of cultural relativism: how to react to a cultural practice that is utterly abhorrent to us, but is part of the lives of those who practise it – in this case eating human flesh. He responds with a statement that sums up in one sentence all that I have been saying:

'It does not sadden me that we should note the horrible barbarity in a practice such as theirs: what does sadden me is that, while judging correctly of their wrong-doings we should be so blind to our own.'

I hope that you will want to argue about some of the points that I have raised. Thank you for giving me the opportunity to raise them and good luck for the rest of your conference.

Conference of Nordic IB Schools, Herlufsholm, Denmark, September 2001

Our shared humanity: developing an international conscience

'One cannot consort with birds and beasts. If I do not associate with humankind, with whom shall I associate?'

Confucius (552-479 BC)

'… while we live, while we are among human beings, let us cultivate our humanity.'

Seneca (2 BC-65 AD)

Introduction

When I decided to make my career in education, first as a science teacher, next as a university lecturer, then as a headmaster and now with the IBO, I knew that two things were certain – I would never make much money but I would never be asked to justify my decision. And so it has proved: the absence of riches has been more than balanced by the constant stimulus of the job and by the knowledge that, whatever the frustrations, it has always been so obviously worthwhile. No one ever asks me the question, 'whatever made you decide to go into education?' and I am arrogant enough to believe that George Bernard Shaw's aphorism, 'those who can, do; those who can't, teach' did not apply to me!

To be appointed Director General of the International School of Geneva, a school of more than 3000 students of 120 different nationalities, offering programmes in French and English, was to have one of the best jobs in the world of education. But eight years later the move to the IBO seemed entirely logical and has indeed proved every bit as stimulating. It is not just a question of the intellectual challenge, or the opportunity to work with outstanding colleagues and to travel to places I never dreamed I would visit. It is to be at the heart of an organization that has a purpose which is expressed not just as a goal, but as an *ideal*.

I see the practical commitment to that ideal expressed in different ways, for example, in our programmes, in the material evidence that supports the applications of schools for authorization, in the very special atmosphere at conferences and workshops, in the different schools that I visit around the world and perhaps most especially in the quality of our students.

But I believe we cannot take the understanding and the sharing of that ideal for granted; from time to time we need to examine it carefully and ask just what its different components mean and how we intend to go about achieving them. And that is what I wish to do today because I regard this as my particular responsibility and it forms part of a deliberate process that I started soon after my appointment in 1999. Two years ago, at the annual meeting of the Council of Foundation in Budapest, I took the opportunity to lay out what I understand by an 'international education'. Since then, at different conferences and workshops in Oman, Accra, Bath and Prague, and in the pages of the *International Schools Journal*, I have tried to look in more detail at each of the different components and today's keynote address will complete the first phase of what has been an ongoing, and will be a never-ending, process.

I therefore make no apology for starting with the IBO's mission statement. It is a strange document, recently described by a journalist, unkindly but correctly, as the obvious product of a committee. But despite its length, its inelegance and its rather obvious desire to please everyone, I keep returning to it as a source of renewal and inspiration. If it does nothing else, it explains how the IBO is different. Here it is:

> 'Through comprehensive and balanced curricula coupled with challenging assessments, the International Baccalaureate Organization aims to assist schools in their endeavours to develop the individual talents of young people and teach them to relate the experience of the classroom to the realities of the world outside. Beyond intellectual rigour and high academic standards, strong emphasis is placed on the ideals of international understanding and responsible citizenship, to the end that IB students may become critical and compassionate thinkers, lifelong learners and informed participants in local and world affairs, conscious of the shared humanity that binds all people together while respecting the variety of cultures and attitudes that makes for the richness of life.'

The component that I want to examine with you today is that phrase 'the shared humanity that binds all people together'. What is it that we all have in common; what do we share that brings us together as human beings, transcending our differences and making us all citizens of the world? Because at present, in most parts of the world, we seem much more inclined to draw attention to our differences than to acknowledge that we all come from a common ancestral stock.

In saying that I am not just thinking of the appalling acts of inhumanity that man (and, in this context, I do largely mean 'man') is capable of inflicting upon other human beings: the historic persecution of the Jews and the Huguenots, the slave trade, the recent ethnic cleansing of parts of the Balkans and systematic genocide in countries in central Africa. Nor do I have in mind the extraordinary situation that I found myself in more than 30 years ago when I spent a year studying in South Africa. Hendrik Verwoerd was prime minister, Nelson Mandela was imprisoned not far away on Robben Island and the greater part of a whole nation had been defined by church and state as belonging to a different part of humanity to mine. Such was the unmistakable message of apartheid.

No: I am thinking more of the daily acts that occur in every multicultural society that exclude rather than include other people by emphasizing what is *different*, which might be colour, language, custom or religion, compared to what is the *same*, which is our 'shared humanity'. I am guilty of this every time I go through customs and immigration in a European airport when instinctively I choose the queue with the fewest black faces because I know these people will hold us all up when they are stopped for lengthy questioning.

Perhaps if we can understand that phrase 'our shared humanity' a little better, we shall be able to help our students to translate it more readily into their everyday lives. I do not promise you an easy ride in the next few minutes but I imagine you did not invite me to come all this way in order to amuse you or to offer you some dubious package of educational tricks. Instead I want us to exercise our minds, and we are going to start back in classical times, because the idea we are exploring is not new.

Act 1: The citizen of the world

Socrates, who died in 399 BC, promoted the concept of the 'examined life'. He accepted only the authority of human reason and encouraged his students to take an intellectual scalpel even to the most traditional wisdom. It sounds just like a good Theory of Knowledge lesson, but for many of those taking part at the time concepts of moral duty, truth and justice would become matters of life or death, not least for Socrates himself who was condemned to death for his intellectual corruption of the young. For Socrates, then, the capacity to reason and the ability to defend opinions by reasoned argument were the most distinctive human qualities; these were the true expression of humanity.

The philosophers known as the Cynics admired Socrates and it was Diogenes (yes, he who lived in a tub and died in 423 BC) who first used the phrase 'citizen of the world'. Today, the word 'cosmopolitan' brings to mind a rather glossy magazine and an international lifestyle that it reflects. But the word is Greek (*kosmou* and *polites*) and it means 'world citizen'. Only by stepping outside our own familiar assumptions by becoming cosmopolitan, argues Diogenes, can we truly question and thereby better understand our own way of life. Diogenes took the challenge of Socrates a step further by adopting a lifestyle, as well as a teaching style, that challenged convention. His famous encounter with Alexander the Great, whom he told to stop blocking the sun, seems to typify his public behaviour but Diogenes' unpopularity and Socrates' death remind us that freedom of speech and of argument were not easily won and will never be easily defended.

The Stoics became the more respectable face of cynicism and the Roman statesman, Seneca, who died in 65 AD, wrote (and so far as we know neither Socrates nor Diogenes wrote anything) that education must develop within us a sense of belonging both to a world community and to the community of our birth. We only understand ourselves in relation to other reasonable people who think and behave differently to us. Local factions, loyalties and cliques (which bedevilled the politics of Seneca's Rome) will constrain our imagination and cause damage to the greater good.

Of course, it could be argued that the concept of 'the world' 2000 years ago was significantly different to that of today, but let us not forget that the empires of Alexander and the Romans covered huge areas of the globe and embraced peoples of widely differing appearances, customs and traditions. The debates going on in Athens and Rome were more than just intellectual mind-sharpening.

For me, three main themes emerge from this brief glimpse at classical philosophy:

- humanity is defined as the human ability to reason

- a human being will understand him/herself better in comparison with other, different human beings

- human beings have both a local and a global responsibility and these ideas built the earliest foundation of what we can describe today as an 'international conscience': the theme of our conference.

Predictably, I have already mentioned the Theory of Knowledge component of the IB Diploma Programme. But let me also suggest that Socrates,

Diogenes and Seneca would have found themselves entirely at home with our Primary Years Programme. For example, the six transdisciplinary themes:

- who we are
- where we are in place and time
- how we express ourselves
- how the world works
- how we organize ourselves
- sharing the planet

provide a sound framework for the development within our students of those three characteristics that I mentioned earlier: the capacity to reason, a knowledge of others and a growing sense of global responsibility.

The first interlude

Let us leave classical times (Nussbaum, 1997) and in a moment re-appear a little nearer to our own time. But first I want to tell you a story.

In the early 1950s a concert of classical music was broadcast live one evening from the studios of the Soviet radio station in Moscow. It was given by one of Russia's finest symphony orchestras with a conductor and soloist of international repute. The concert went well and as they disbanded everyone agreed that the performance of Mozart's piano concerto in D minor, K466 had been unusually fine.

Someone else agreed too because the following morning the producer took a telephone call from Stalin. He had listened to the concert and had particularly enjoyed the Mozart, so much so that he would like to have a copy of the tape. The producer went to organize it, only to discover to his dismay, indeed to his horror, that the recording equipment had not functioned properly and the tape was distorted beyond repair. Two cardinal sins had been committed: Stalin's wish could not be satisfied and, even worse, he would learn that the station's essential monitoring equipment was not functioning efficiently.

There was only one solution. The orchestra was immediately reassembled with the conductor who was still in Moscow; the soloist was summoned back from Japan and the concerto performed a second time. Stalin was very pleased to receive the tape. But that is not the end of the story. About a year later, he died and by his bedside was found a tape recorder containing this very tape.

This, of course, is a cautionary tale. How could one of the most evil mass murderers in history have loved Mozart, indeed loved Mozart at his most perplexing in this particular concerto? The lesson is simple if hard to accept: history shows us that a person's humanity towards others has very little to do with being cultured, having a warm, attractive personality or a love of this book or that painting. Diogenes seems to have had none of those qualities but, unlike Josef Stalin, he had the beginnings of an international conscience.

Act 2: Living together

Despite my earlier comments about the Alexandrian and Roman empires, it is self-evident that today's global village appears very different to any possible conception of the world viewed from ancient Greece or Rome. Today, the need for peaceful coexistence has never been more urgent as the choice of moving somewhere else, except as a reluctant refugee, has disappeared. Sharing our humanity has now become a matter of life and death and the last century should be marked as the period when the very worst behaviour of humankind eventually provoked the very best response in the creation of global institutions like the United Nations and sister organizations such as the World Health Organization, the International Labour Organization, the High Commission for Refugees and so on. Let us not forget, either, that they were all modelled on an earlier Swiss example, the International Red Cross.

Imperfect though they are, they represent a formidable, tangible expression of our desire to share our humanity and those early philosophers could have written the ringing words that introduce the constitution of UNESCO, the international organization for education with which the IBO has an important consultative status:

> 'Since wars begin in the minds of men, it is in the minds of men that the defences of peace must be constructed.

> 'Ignorance of each other's ways and lives has been a common cause, throughout the history of mankind, of that suspicion and mistrust between the peoples of the world through which their differences have too often broken into war.'

One person in particular bridges the gap between the ancient philosophers' concept of the world citizen and the ideal of working together through organizations of international cooperation: the German philosopher, Immanuel Kant. Don't worry: even if I could, I am not going to embark on a detailed analysis of the writings of a notoriously complex philosopher. But what is the point of philosophy if reasonably intelligent people cannot grasp its essentials, even in a form that might cause the professional philosopher to wince?

Kant (who died in 1804) was greatly influenced by the Stoics in his search for a moral system based upon universal principles. Like Socrates, he was convinced that the greatest human quality was rationality and its application in the exercise of moral duty. Kant's three categorical imperatives are especially relevant to our theme:

- to be acceptable, any individual moral action should have universal application

- human beings should never be treated only as means, but as ends

- human beings ought to, and as rational beings do, extend the rule of law.

The first of these three imperatives is sometimes loosely translated as 'do unto others as you would have them do unto you' and it introduces a concept that is fundamental to any understanding of our shared humanity, that of empathy – the ability to understand and share the feelings of another. If I may digress just for a moment, I cannot resist noting that the longer I live with two dogs, albeit two particularly intelligent dogs, the more I come to question any clear distinction between human and animal characteristics. The number of qualities that are uniquely human is, I suspect, rather small but one of them is certainly empathy – the ability to put yourself into another's place and ask how it really feels.

My good friend David Wilkinson, headmaster of Mahindra United World College in India, drew my attention to the following passage from George Orwell's *The Road to Wigan Pier*. Orwell was returning home from visiting a town in the North of England when he noticed from the train window a young woman unblocking a pipe at the rear of her terraced house. He wrote:

'She looked up as the train passed and I was almost near enough to catch her eye. She had a round pale face, the usual exhausted face of the slum dweller who is twenty-five and looks forty... It struck me that we are mistaken when we say "it isn't the same for them as it would be for us"... she knew well enough what was happening to her and understood as well as I did how dreadful a destiny it was to be kneeling there in bitter cold on the slimy stones of a slum backyard poking a stick up a foul drain pipe.'

(Orwell, 1936)

This episode illustrates true empathy: not merely asking what it would be like standing there in the slum courtyard (cold, wet and smelly) but recognizing the actual feelings of that woman trapped in such a situation (depression, hopelessness, perhaps a spark of determination). Empathy is not putting you, yourself into another's situation, but trying to become her, herself in that situation and it is not easy.

I cannot leave Kant without a passing glimpse at the other two imperatives which, incidentally, some would insist are merely different statements of the first. The second introduces the concept of human dignity which is a very good litmus test of a human situation that is going badly wrong. When a person's humanity is being affronted, an immediate effect is a perceptible loss of human dignity. We see it in the small child being humiliated in front of the class, in those travellers undergoing interrogation in the immigration queue as well as in the indelible images of Jews scrubbing pre-war German pavements and being herded into train carriages like animals.

The third imperative takes us straight back to Socrates. Human beings can act rationally, says Kant, and will act rationally when it becomes clear that it is in their best interests to do so. The rule of law brings good to a greater number of people than the rule of anarchy. This is common sense, which means literally that it is founded upon a shared human understanding. In a remarkable essay called 'Perpetual Peace' (Kant, 1795) written in his old age, Kant developed his optimism in the ability of human beings to use their common sense to avoid war and he actually proposed the formation of a 'league of nations':

> '… establish a continuously growing state consisting of various nations which will ultimately include all the nations of the world… This league does not tend to any domination over the power of the state but only to the maintenance and security of the freedom of the state itself and of other states in league with it.'

Let us note, with some satisfaction, that Stalin would have failed all three of Kant's imperatives (most notably the second), so with this added confidence we can put on our list three more important themes concerning our shared humanity:

- education must help human beings to develop the capacity of empathy
- the lives of human beings must never be used as means to an end
- we must educate human beings to have belief in the rational abilities of themselves and others.

The second interlude

At this point I think you have earned a break so here is another story that will end up closer to home, here in Australia. Some time ago I was reading the original account of one of the earliest explorations in the Arctic. A Royal Naval expedition, led by Commander John Ross, was searching for the North West passage in 1818 and, like most expeditions of that period, it became stuck in the ice, not entirely sure where it was. After a few days, a small group of Polar Inuit (who had been isolated centuries earlier from the main group of Greenland Inuit and believed they were alone in the world) appeared with sledges (Fleming, 1998). Over the next few days there took place one of the most extraordinary encounters in the history of exploration, perhaps unique in that neither side had any intention of exploiting the other. The British simply wanted to know where they were; the Inuit wanted to know whether this extraordinary group, which descended onto the ice in full naval dress, had any possible human connection with them. The Inuit believed the ships with their moving sails and rigging were animate, probably from the sun or the moon. Were the newcomers a race of men, or did they have any women (Ross was obliged to show them his wife's portrait)? What did they make of the pigs and the dogs that the expedition kept on board?

This wonderful account of one group of people sizing up another group for recognizable signs of humanity made me search for other examples. My colleague, Ian Hill, himself a Tasmanian, found for me in the Bibliothèque Nationale de France in Paris the ship's log of the French captain, Nicolas Baudin, whose corvettes, *Geographe* and *Naturaliste*, spent a month off '*La Terre de Van Diemen*' in January 1802. The log is even dated as the month of '*pluviôse*', from the French revolutionary republican calendar! Baudin reports several meetings with groups of '*naturels*', the aboriginals, and a pattern seems to emerge from their different encounters: fear – curiosity – exchange of goods – collaboration – exploration of objects – renewed fear – precautions – protection – exploration of people – renewed fear – exploration of language – first violence.

Each new encounter seems to start from a renewed position of fear. But, on every occasion, peace is restored and the whole episode has a happy ending largely because of the obvious sympathy shown by the French sailors towards the aboriginal children. Baudin's log ends:

> '*au bout d'une heure ou deux ils furent aussi familiarisés avec nous que si nous avions été d'anciennes connaissances.*'

A better known example is the encounter that took place in the Papua New Guinea highlands in the 1930s which was actually filmed by the Leahy brothers. The indigenous people, who were completely unknown outside their isolated valleys, thought the white gold prospectors were the spirits of their dead ancestors and this was further reinforced when the prospectors' light plane landed amongst them. Looking back on these events many years later, an old woman explained, "It was not until we had sex with them that we finally understood the white men were humans."

Act 3: The human condition

Let us leave Immanuel Kant behind at the beginning of the 19th century and move on 150 years to the end of the Second World War and to another tough nut to crack, the French philosopher Jean-Paul Sartre. In 1945 Sartre, recently released from imprisonment for his resistance activities, gave a lecture in Paris entitled 'Existentialism and Humanism' in which he explained the relationship between the two concepts (Sartre, 1973). The existentialists insist that there is no such thing as an 'essence of humanity' on which different human beings are modelled. Rejecting Kant's assumption of 'what human beings are like', Sartre insists that they are only 'what they decide to become' which is a very different matter, not least in its implications for their teachers.

It is a particularly significant lecture from our point of view because Sartre, while rejecting a universal essence called 'human nature' does accept a universality of the 'human condition'. Every human being, he argues, knows what it is like to operate within the limitations imposed by survival on this planet and therefore each of us, whatever our cultural background, can understand another's purposes because it will be to accept, overcome or modify these limitations. In a famous passage, he writes:

> 'Consequently, every purpose, however individual it may be, is of universal value. Every purpose, even that of a Chinese, an Indian or a Negro (*sic*) can be understood by a European.'

Despite the encouragement that passage gives to the idea of an international conscience, Sartre's message seems bleak: is the human condition no more than a question of survival? In fact this is *not* Sartre's message because he qualifies this basic condition with the possibility of redefining the limitations beyond mere survival, but how far is he prepared to go?

Someone who can shed some light on this question is the American psychologist, Abraham Maslow, who died in 1970 (Wikipedia, 2006). Maslow proposed a hierarchy of human needs:

- physiological (food, water, warmth)
- safety
- a sense of belonging
- esteem
- self-fulfilment
- satisfying curiosity

each level of which can be reached only when the previous level has been satisfied. Maslow called the earlier four levels 'deficiency motivation' and suggested that only when these basic deficiency needs have been satisfied will the person achieve 'self-actualization' or personal autonomy.

One of the problems about the concept of 'a shared humanity' is the gross inequality of levels of the human condition that are experienced by different peoples around the world. Maslow's model translates into a very steep pyramid within which huge numbers of people are imprisoned at ground level searching desperately for adequate food, water and warmth. In terms of education, the statistics make the point very clearly:

- in the Arab States one in four children (10.3 million) is out of primary school
- in Europe there is 100% coverage of primary education
- 42 million children do not attend primary school in sub-Saharan Africa
- 95% of children in Latin America and the Caribbean attend primary school.

Perhaps the most dangerous aspect of all this, for those of us who are fortunate enough to operate somewhere near the pinnacle of Maslow's pyramid of needs, is the unspoken assumption that the situation will never change, at least not in our lifetime. In sending me that passage from George Orwell, David Wilkinson added his own personal comment:

> 'Over 60 years has gone by (since Orwell's quote) and I watch the women in the paddy fields and wonder what has happened in all that time.'

So let us not fall into the trap of treating material deprivation as an inescapable consequence of cultural diversity as though, given the choice, those Indian women would wish to remain working in the paddy fields any more than Orwell's woman would have wished to remain confined to her slum.

The statistics can appear so depressing that it is tempting to go away and think about something else, yet if minds were focused (and UNESCO is indeed trying to focus them through its Education for All initiative) significant progress could be made (UNESCO, 2006). Imagine, for example, there were universal agreement that the Earth was going to be hit by an asteroid of modest size in exactly two years' time. Would not every resource on the planet be devoted to a concerted, cooperative attempt to avert the catastrophe? Is the current state of education around the globe significantly different in the scope of its potential danger?

Before I sum up, I think we can now add three more aspects of our understanding of shared humanity which stem from the work of Sartre and Maslow:

- despite our very different cultural backgrounds, there is a level at which we all share an understanding of the human condition

- the level of this understanding will depend upon our relative positions on a scale of satisfied human needs

- for too many human beings on this planet, that level is still the basic one of daily survival.

Conclusion

It is time to sum up so let me first repeat the list of nine elements that we have identified as contributing to our understanding of the concept of a 'shared humanity':

1. humanity is defined as the human ability to reason

2. a human being will understand him/herself better in comparison with other, different human beings

3. human beings have both a local and a global responsibility

4. education must help human beings to develop the capacity of empathy

5. the lives of human beings must never be used as means to an end

6. we must educate human beings to have belief in the rational abilities of themselves and of others

7. despite our very different cultural backgrounds, there is a level at which we all share an understanding of the human condition

8. the level of this understanding will depend upon our relative positions on a scale of satisfied human needs

9. for too many human beings on this planet, that level is still the basic one of daily survival.

Each of these elements, I suggest, contributes to the development of an international conscience: a moral sense of what is right and what is wrong that takes into account those who live beyond our village, our region and our nation. One challenge to the IBO – and I hope this will be the subject of your discussions during this conference – is to relate the first six of these elements to our three programmes. A different, but related, challenge is to ask what contribution the IBO can make to the last three elements and that is, indeed, something that we are trying to address.

During this talk we have travelled across the globe: from Josef Stalin in Moscow to Abraham Maslow (who was the son of Russian Jewish immigrants) in the United States; from Commander Ross in the Arctic to Captain Baudin in Tasmania. Immanuel Kant, however, was born in Königsberg and he died 80 years later in Königsberg from where he had scarcely moved during his entire lifetime. Let us be quite clear that an international conscience does not require an international airport.

But if Kant did not move, Königsberg did: from Prussia to Poland to Germany to a 'Polish corridor' to the Soviet Union, renamed Kaliningrad, and then to the Russian Federation where today it is an enclave designated as a special economic zone. There is a movement that would have it become the fourth independent Baltic state.

The human misery associated with that small area of land with its million-and-a-half inhabitants illustrates better than any philosophical treatise the importance of developing a shared humanity and an international conscience.

> To see the earth as it truly is
> small and blue and beautiful
> in that eternal silence where it floats,
> is to see ourselves
> as riders on the earth together,
> brothers on that bright loveliness in the eternal cold –
> brothers who know now they are truly brothers.

(Macleish, 1968)

Conference of the Australian Association of IB Schools,
Melbourne, Australia, July 2001

References

Fleming, F. (1998) *Barrow's Boys*. Granta Books.

Kant, I. (1795) *Zum ewigen Frieden.*

Macleish, A. (1968) Riders on Earth, Brothers in Eternal Cold. *New York Times,* 25 December. Reprinted in *Riders on the Earth*, Houghton Mifflin Co, 1978.

Nussbaum, M. (1997) *Cultivating Humanity*. Harvard University Press.

Orwell, G (1936) *The Road to Wigan Pier*. Harcourt Inc.

Sartre, J P. (1973) *Existentialism and Humanism*. Trans. P Mairet. Methuen, London.

UNESCO. (Accessed July 2006) www.unesco.org/education/efa/ed_for_all/index.shtml

Wikipedia (Acccessed July 2006) http://en.wikipedia.org/wiki/Abraham_Maslow

"At the same time, a stable society can only be constructed from a strong measure of shared understanding..."

The next article is a second revision of a lecture that I first gave in 1999. The topic – the search for a set of universal values to which all nations will subscribe – is one that quickly polarizes opinions. Cultural relativists will say it is doomed to failure but the global citizen believes the search is in itself a worthwhile exercise that will lead to better understanding.

The revised nature of this lecture reflects my own struggle with the topic.

The search for universal values

You talk of Ultimate Value, Universal Form –
Visions, let me tell you, that ride upon the storm
And must be made and sought but cannot be maintained,
Lost as soon as caught, always to be regained,
Mainstream of our striving towards perfection.

From 'Plurality' by Louis MacNeice (1940)

How can Atlas support the world?

One of the most stimulating essays on international education was written by Grey Mattern in Jonietz and Harris (1991) with the misleadingly whimsical title 'Random ruminations on the curriculum of the international school'. In a classroom containing many different nationalities, cultures and languages, asks Mattern, what is holding up the world? What is the common denominator of all this apparent human diversity? On what moral foundation does Atlas stand in order to support the whole world, not just chosen parts of it?

> 'At its heart lies a word which, except in its mathematical sense, has been banished from most of the institutions purporting to give such an education: the word is values. It is banished because schools do not want to display bias. They do not want to imply, unless something can be held up to some universally accepted (and thus 'objective') measuring rod, anything is better than, worth more than, in any way exceeds in value anything else.'

So Mattern deplores the reluctance of schools to discuss values lest cultural feathers become ruffled because he believes that certain values 'are and have been common to every civilization past and present'. For example:

- Every ethical system holds firmly to the importance of truth-telling
- Every ethical system teaches the importance of respect for the rights of others and of systems which maintain this
- Virtually every nation on earth lays claim to being a democracy
- Every society values respect and benevolence between human beings.

One must admire the way Mattern plunges headfirst into a topic that provokes controversy, disagreement and polarization, illustrated at the extreme by the two contrasting statements:

> 'We must have the courage to think globally, to break away from traditional paradigms and plunge boldly into the unknown. We must so mobilise our inner and outer resources that we begin consciously to build a new world based on mutually assured welfare rather than mutually assured destruction.' (Singh in UNESCO, 1996)

> 'Standards of rationality and right conduct are neither independent of particular cultural contexts nor commensurable as between cultures: they are culture bound.' (Zec, 1980)

Unfortunately, Mattern's rather shaky choice of metaphor (in Greek mythology, Atlas was condemned by Zeus to hold up the heavens not the earth) is followed by his dubious choice of example. A moment's reflection, based upon recent world events, warns us that universally agreed concepts like 'the rights of others' and 'respect and benevolence' are open to very different cultural interpretations. Even 'truth' and 'democracy' have quite different meanings amongst different cultures. I am reminded, for example, that the South African Truth and Reconciliation Commission defined four kinds of truth: factual and objective truth, narrative truth, including 'perceptions, stories and myths', social truth 'established by discussion and debate' and restorative truth 'healing victims by securing a public acknowledgement of their suffering'. (Jeffery, 1999). In his bold prediction about democracy:

> 'From now on the values of democracy will be part of humanity's common heritage. This heritage will need protection because it is fragile and progress in democracy is often followed by retreat.'

Mayor, the then director general of UNESCO (1998), was no doubt encouraged by the unravelling of the Soviet empire but more recent experience in Afghanistan, Iraq and Palestine suggests that values assumed in the West's interpretation of democracy may not be universally shared.

Nonetheless, if Mattern's essay uncovers the problems rather than suggests their solutions, it serves to focus our minds on what is perhaps the most important challenge for the international educator: what assumptions can we reasonably make about the way other groups of people ought to behave? At heart, what values do we all have in common?

Human values

Values have been defined (Oxford English Dictionary) as 'one's principles or standards, one's judgment of what is valuable or important in life.' They have been described by Hofstede (1991) as 'broad tendencies to prefer certain states of affairs over others. Values are feelings with an arrow to it: they have a plus and a minus side' and they are at the heart of our culture. Although we experience only the external manifestations, for example, the well-loved rituals, the symbols and the heroes, these are the symptoms of what lies underneath: deeply held convictions about what is worthwhile and what is important in life. Defending their values is what people die for.

Values are not inherited; they are learned and that is why they are of particular interest to educators. Moreover, all the evidence suggests they are learned at an early age. However, values have not always been explicitly taught; it was often assumed they would be acquired by more informal interactions, and the so-called *hidden curriculum* of a school (for example, the way its teachers behave towards their students and towards each other) is reckoned to be just as influential as the formal curriculum. This will have been the personal experience of many of us: long after all those timetabled lessons have been forgotten, the personal examples of our teachers and our fellow students have remained with us as powerful models. These people, and of course to an even greater extent our family, were helping us to acquire our values.

But in many schools today the values curriculum is no longer hidden; a deliberate attempt is being made to teach them. In the People's Republic of China young people will be taught five loves: for the motherland, the people, work, science and the socialist system. In Vietnam, values education is based on four categories of ethics: individual, man to man, man to occupation and man to nature. In Iran, religion is the foundation for the promotion of values. In the West it will probably be called *personal and social education* or *education for citizenship* but, although titles and motives will differ, schools around the world are unashamedly trying to inculcate certain values in their students.

The International Baccalaureate Organization (2005) has published an 'IB learner profile' which lists ten desired characteristics of internationally minded young people. The list can leave no doubt in the minds of the teacher that certain values – *they are courageous... they have integrity, honesty... they show empathy, compassion and respect... they have a sound grasp on the principles of moral reasoning... they are open to the perspectives, values and traditions of other individuals and cultures* – are to be made explicit and treated as a key element of all teaching strategies.

Understanding the values of another cultural group is a huge challenge; indeed the cultural relativists insist that it is not possible. But should we remain silent in the face of the Taliban who restricted girls' access to education; Indian women who abort female foetuses; the still widespread ritual of female circumcision in many African countries; the virtually unrestricted access to firearms in the United States? As a first step, we must try to understand why a group still believes that a particular practice is important to its cultural identity, indeed even to its cultural survival. We might call this a *meeting of minds*, but understanding should not be confused with agreement. We need not accept the cultural relativists' position which, in its final logic, implies that *anything goes*, including cannibalism and human sacrifice. But it is only from a foundation of understanding that justifiable criticism can be launched.

Cultural Relativism

According to Zaw (1996):

> 'The cultural relativist argument runs as follows. Values are meaningful only within a particular culture. Therefore the conception of absolute or culture-neutral values is a contradiction in terms. It follows that the value-system of one culture cannot be rationally regarded as absolutely better than that of another, since no culture-neutral standpoint is philosophically available from which the values of different cultures are intelligible, let alone susceptible of impartial comparison and rational judgement by the standards of absolute value.'

This implies a dead end in our search but can we not seek a way out of the impasse by agreeing that some human needs are universal? Sartre has explored the universality of the 'human condition':

> 'What never vary,' writes Sartre (1945) 'are the necessities of being in the world, of having to labour and to die there... And diverse though man's purposes may be, at least none of them is wholly foreign to me... '

and the experiences of the earliest explorers remind us how much of 'man's purposes' were immediately obvious to groups of people who shared little except their common human appearance.

This approach allows us to argue that universal needs must create universal values. It is not difficult to identify some of them: the United Nations Universal Declaration of Human Rights (1948) looks forward to a world:

'… in which human beings shall enjoy freedom of speech and belief and freedom from fear and want.'

But now another difficulty arises as different cultures attach a different 'value' to what we are claiming to be a universal principle. For example, the violent controversy that developed in 2006 following the publication in European journals of cartoons deemed to be insulting to Islam caused an uncomfortable juxtaposition of the freedom of speech and the freedom of belief. Different groups attached a different value to one compared to the other. Perhaps it is therefore helpful to think also of a 'value' actually in its numerical sense; we can agree to share a set of values but have significantly different interpretations of their priority.

To give another example, the return of Hong Kong from Britain to China was bedevilled by hugely different perceptions of democracy. The last British Governor, Chris Patten, who was fiercely criticised for his unbending approach to the Chinese over democratic ideals, commented sarcastically to a British Parliamentary Committee:

'"Well, our price is slaughter of the first born. That's not unreasonable in the circumstances, you have to allow for cultural tradition." I mean, do we ever have a bottom line?'

Dimbleby (1997)

A further example is provided by the dilemma of the Muslim girl described in Zaw (1996). She is attending a British state school and when she reaches adolescence, her parents write to the headmaster asking that she be excluded from all school activities that might bring her into physical proximity to boys. The girl herself begs the head to ignore her parents' wishes, but he knows that this will make them withdraw the girl from the school altogether.

None of these cases implies the outright rejection of a value – freedom of speech, democratic politics or the right to education – but each case rates one value as less important than another. When pushed to the limit, the girl's parents would rather sacrifice her education than compromise their religious beliefs. What is essential here is the need to understand the other person's values and to be willing to try to negotiate a new position that is mutually acceptable so that neither person is pushed to the limit.

Universal or Western values?

'In order to maintain Jordan's international position, we have to accept that not to become a player in the global village is to commit economic suicide. In effect, all graduates have to be qualified internationally in order best to serve their patriotic interests. How do we do this and still maintain our cultural identity?'

That recent statement by a young Jordanian teacher articulates the sense of loss, the sense of regret, the sense of uncertainty that is felt by people around the world who believe they are being forced to compromise their cultural values in order to succeed in an economic race driven by Western capitalism. If they are to avoid becoming endangered cultural species they have no choice but to compete, but the nature and demands of the competition seem likely to threaten the very cultural identity they are seeking to protect.

The Chinese academic, Professor Zhou Nanzhao, writing in a personal capacity in UNESCO (1996) lists the strengths (which include valuing education, having high expectations, emphasizing the group rather than the individual) and the weaknesses (which include a disdain for pragmatism, utilitarianism and business, an over-emphasis on classics-oriented examinations and gender bias) of Asian cultures. Significantly, he focuses on those values that will benefit the achievement of economic goals and thus maintain Asia's competitive position in a globalized market rather than those that might, for example, contribute to the enrichment of the arts, to alternative medicine or to a healthier, more balanced lifestyle.

Friedman (2005) warns the United States and Europe of the economic challenge posed by new global players, notably China and India, but it is apparent that their success is due to their ability to exploit the globalized economy even more efficiently – partly because of cheap labour – than the West. They have taken on the West at its own game and they are starting to win. Meanwhile, an increasing number of groups that either cannot or will not join the game (many of them in rural areas) are taking to the streets in violent protest. Jacques (2006) writes:

'By the end of this century Europe is likely to pale into insignificance alongside China and India. In such a world, Europe will be forced to observe and respect the sensibilities of others.'

but he does not ask at what cultural price this battle will be won and what sensibilities might be left to respect in the possibly deeply divided Chinese and Indian communities.

Reverting to type

In 1999, NATO aircraft controversially bombed Kosovo in order to force a withdrawal of Serbian forces from that area of Yugoslavia. As often happens in moments of international crisis, the alumni of the world's oldest international school, the International School of Geneva (Ecolint), turned to their online chat service. What follows is the exact transcript of part of a long debate, reprinted with the author's permission. It requires neither explanation nor comment, but it illustrates how readily the three students, S, A and R, seem to have abandoned the international values that their privileged education had instilled in them and reverted to national, even nationalist, stereotype. At the same time we need to note that, unlike these three, the author has no personal connection with the Balkan region.

'There have been some pretty remarkable things said of late by members of this network. I'd have to say that the future looks fairly dim, if some of these voices are those of people who claim cultural and national blindness in the selection of their friends, or who claim to adhere to an internationalist view instilled at least in part by their Ecolint experience.

'Perhaps the problem arises when that enlightened perspective collides with a greater force. Tradition. By all means let's honour tradition. Because our great-grandfathers were racists, let's be racists. Because our mothers held in distaste those of other ethnic backgrounds, let's do the same. Because our priests and ministers and rabbis and ayatollahs teach that only our way is true, let's hold in disdain those who follow a different path. And by all means, because someone wronged our grandfathers, let's cling to that long-past trespass and hate the sons and granddaughters of that wrongdoer, however innocent they may be. Did our parents offer us nothing to give to our children but the hatreds and resentments and fears which their parents gave to them?

'I am appalled and disgusted by S's suggestion that Belgrade be carpet-bombed, not to mention the fact that this is presented as the "civilized" response. Perhaps he doesn't know what carpet-bombing is, or how indiscriminate it is. I am equally disgusted by the suggestion that Milosevic merits support now because blessed Serbia is being bombed. What, my Serb friends, would Milosevic have to do, how far would he have to go before you would say "No. No more. I am a member of the family of humankind first, and a Serb a distant second. It must stop, it must stop with this generation, it must stop today." What would it take?

'In S's laying claim to a civilized status, he further argues that NATO action in Kosovo is a manifestation of the world keeping its vow to prevent another holocaust. "Never again." That vow was broken before the echoes of the bombs of World War II faded. There have been agains and agains and agains. Where were the civilized when Stalin filled the Gulag with camps and corpses? Where were the civilized when Pol Pot murdered Cambodia? Where were the civilized when Augusto Pinochet disappeared thousands? Where were the civilized when generations of South Africans were oppressed, murdered, displaced? Where were the civilized when the rivers of Rwanda flowed red? Where have the civilized been as Palestinians have blown buses to bits and Israelis have bulldozed the homes of grandmothers? Where are the civilized as children starve and the United States builds weapons with money that could buy bread? Where is the civilization in arguing against saving innocents because "our interests are not threatened?" What greater interest can a civilized society have than the survival of other human beings?

'A spoke much about the past. He obviously feels that there have been many wrongs that have gone unaddressed, and certainly history is filled with evidence to support that feeling. Many wrongs, committed by many and suffered by many more. While I may be sorry that A's Grandfather suffered, the defining feature of his story is that it is history. We cannot make A's Grandfather's life whole. A retells the story of Croatian and Albanian collaboration with the Nazis, as though, 55 years on, some sort of retaliation is justified. But against whom? The children who live in Kosovo today? Their young mothers and fathers? Through how many generations does the stain of a sin survive?

'R argues that "Kosovo is the birthplace of Serbia and the Serbian Orthodox religion, and therefore Albanian independence is entirely out of the question, and autonomy is highly undesirable." Why? What difference does it make? Are your god and your faith so fragile that they exist only by dint of possession of a plot of ground? Is your self-identity so brittle and narrowly defined? In a similar vein, A drew a parallel between Jerusalem and Kosovo. Kosovo and Jerusalem – better they should never have existed, when what their existence has led to over the centuries is dispute and hatred and division. If good once existed there, if glories once were seen, they have been dragged through the filth by generations of small minds who have twisted and tortured what may have been good, or who have kept alive what should have been forgotten, for use as petty arguments for possession at any cost and – apparently at least as importantly – for the exclusion of "the other".

'A talks about "cultural incompatibility" and high Albanian birth rates (an observation made about blacks by whites in the United States, about Catholics by Protestants, about Jews by Nazis, the poor by the rich). You're in good company, A, in seeing this as a cause for concern. He also mentions that "Milosevic was elected President." Should we take the fact that Adolf Hitler was elected Chancellor of Germany as an amnesty for his administration?

'Are the Serbian people complicitous, as S said? Of course they are, as is everyone on this list. We are complicitous each and every time we profess belief in a religious construct which says that "We are saved. They are not". Or, even more to the point, that says that no matter what you do to your fellow human beings, paradise can still be yours. What kind of god can forgive a life of brutality by dint of a last-minute apology and profession of devotion, not to humankind but to him/her/it/them? I should think that any just god would see to it that such wicked people leave this life in shame and terror.

'We are complicitous when we wave our respective national flags and puff up our chests and sing our anthems and do everything we can to ensure that we will keep ours, and let those others fend for themselves. We are complicitous when we ally with devils who oppress and murder but who tell us that our enemy is their enemy. We are complicitous when we forget that we are all in this life together, and that what we have in common is certainly far, far greater than what differences there may be.

'When does this damnable hostility end? You, A. You stop it. Do not participate. You, R. You, S. All of you. Take no pride in being born Serbian or French or Colombian or Indian or a citizen of the United States. That you were born what you are is nothing more than an accident. What was accomplished by those who have gone before you is nothing to do with you. You may as well take pride in being tall, or in being blonde, or in being black or white. It is not your doing. What you are truly entitled to take pride in is what you – and only you – have done with your life. If you feel pride in keeping alive the petty ignorances and prejudices of those who have gone before, then yours will be a very small life.'

DA, class of '68'

Universal values

We have noted how the words that describe some apparently basic human values are open to different interpretations. We have also noted how different cultures will attribute a different priority to the same value: some, for example, placing loyalty above honesty, others valuing economic survival more than human rights. If it is difficult to agree on specific words and definitions, can we seek a set of principles from which a code of acceptable behaviour might be derived?

The German philosopher, Immanuel Kant (1724-1804), expressed three such universal principles:

- If an act is right for me, it must be right under the same conditions for everyone ('do as you would be done by')

- Act so as to treat another person as an end and never only as a means (this is one of the greatest moral ideas of the time, ruling out slavery, exploitation, lack of respect for human dignity)

- Human beings ought to, and as rational beings do, extend the rule of law.

He fused together ethics and politics in a remarkable essay entitled '*Zum ewigen Frieden*' ('Perpetual Peace'), written in 1795 when he was 71, in which he even proposed the creation of a 'league of nations':

'This league does not tend to any domination over the power of the state but only to the maintenance and security of the freedom of the state itself and of other states in league with it.'

Two hundred years after Kant, every member state of the United Nations formally signed the Universal Declaration of Human Rights, but the credibility of its watchdog, the Human Rights Commission has been severely weakened by the persistently poor record of some of its member states and its replacement body, a Human Rights Council, awaits the approval of the UN's most powerful member, the United States. Given the complexity of the issues, it is not surprising that international agreement is hard to reach but that is no reason for accepting the *status quo*. If we find it hard to pin down the concept of universal values then we can still accept that one feature of the universal human condition is to question, to challenge and to improve. All human beings can exert their liberty by rejecting the values adopted by others.

Values are maintained or modified in ways that increase the group's chances of survival. At the moment we are seeing a tension developing between the deliberate reinforcement of national and even sub-national values and the growing domination of global imperatives. As we have already noted, the former is partly a reaction to the latter; people are bewildered by economic and political events that seem to move in a sphere that is beyond their experience and control. However, as the global impact of disease, environmental degradation and conflict on our individual lives becomes apparent they, too, will be perceived as a threat to our individual security and we shall have no choice but to take them seriously. Our values will begin to change.

In practice we all belong to different cultural groups: the same person can move comfortably between the school staffroom, the trade union committee and the village football team. In similar fashion, we shall have to learn to operate at a global, a national and a sub-national level because, paradoxically, one of the consequences of globalization has been to increase our awareness of what is local, familiar and easily accommodated.

How can we reconcile different, deeply held cultural values in a shrinking world? I mentioned earlier the essential first step of the *meeting of minds*. It would be comforting to imagine that this would lead, through a process of peaceful negotiation, to an acceptable compromise and then, even though this may take more than a generation, to a *meeting of hearts*. The world is no longer big enough to accommodate isolated cultural groups so we must find ways of living together that retain different cultural identities at a sub-national level while encouraging the national and transnational integration upon which our economic prosperity depends. This is not easy, but many examples exist, where the sub-national diversity is often maintained by linguistic difference and some degree of physical separation. The search continues.

A revision of a lecture first given at the regional conference of
IB Africa, Europe, Middle East, Muscat, Oman, October 1999

References

Dimbleby, J. (1997) *The Last Governor*. London: Little, Brown & Co.

Friedman, T. (2005) *The World is Flat*. London: Allen Lane.

Hofstede, G. (1991) *Cultures and Organizations*. London: Harper Collins.

International Baccalaureate Organization (2005) IB learner profile booklet

Jacques, M. (2006) Europe's contempt for other cultures cannot be sustained, in *The Guardian*, 17 February 2006.

Jeffery, A. (1999) *The Truth about the Truth Commission*. South African Institute of Race Relations.

Jonietz, P. L. & Harris, D. (Eds) (1991) *World Yearbook of Education 1991: International Schools and International Education*. London: Kogan Page.

Sartre, J. P. (1945) *Existentialism and Humanism*. London: Methuen.

UNESCO (1996) *Learning: The Treasure Within*. Paris.

UNESCO (1998) *Quelle démocratie pour le future?* Paris.

Zaw, S. K. (1996) in *Public Education in a Multicultural Society*, R. K. Fullinwinder (Ed.) Cambridge: Cambridge University Press.

Zec, P. (1980) *Journal of Philosophy of Education*, Vol 14 No 1.

"And some of the world's most urgent problems – environmental destruction, poverty and disease – can be solved only through concerted global action."

The article that follows links a great work, *The Social Contract*, of a controversial philosopher, Jean-Jacques Rousseau, to a visionary global organization, The United Nations.

At a time when the UN is under increasing scrutiny, global citizens must recognize that the translation of vision into action requires organizations that function in a manner that commands the widest possible respect and support.

Man is born free

It is both an honour and a pleasure to address you on this 50th anniversary of the Student United Nations (SUN), founded here in Geneva in 1953. The International School of Geneva has contributed much to the world, including the International Baccalaureate, but nothing more important than the SUN of which there are now many imitations across the world. I want to pay tribute to its founder, Robert Leach, and to all the teachers who have supported and developed it up to the present time.

I am at Miami airport, in transit for Mexico. Although I have taken off my coat, then my jacket and then both shoes, the airport security alarm still goes off and I am taken to one side for a full body check which eventually reveals a tiny fragment of aluminium foil in one of my shirt pockets. I am allowed to proceed.

I am left thinking about personal freedom. Here I am in the most democratic of nations, the United States, being subjected to a procedure that one associates with criminals. My personal freedom is being taken away in the cause of a more general freedom that allows me and others to continue to fly despite the ever-present threat of terrorism. No security check: no travel.

Every day that passes seems to bring a further erosion of my personal freedom. To give another example, the Geneva authorities (as in many cities) are making it increasingly difficult to take a private car into the city centre. I am forced to take the tram with these words ringing in my ears: 'Man is born free, and everywhere he is in chains.'

That is the very famous opening line of a very famous book and for the next ten minutes or so I want to talk to you about it. It is arguably the most important book ever written on political philosophy and its author is unarguably Geneva's greatest citizen. I hope to encourage you to read it, and to read about it, because although it is nearly 250 years old, it is as relevant to the 21st century – perhaps even more relevant – as it was to the 18th century when it was written.

The book is called *The Social Contract* (*Du Contrat Social* was the original French title). The author is Jean-Jacques Rousseau. The date is 1762.

Rousseau was born in Geneva but he wrote the book in Paris and it was published in Amsterdam. Copies were immediately burned in the streets of Geneva and a warrant for Rousseau's arrest in France forced him to flee the country.

The controversy surrounding *The Social Contract* continues today. This book inspired America's move to independence. Marat shouted it to the crowds during the French revolution and the Jacobin leader, Robespierre, had Rousseau's ashes moved into the Panthéon in Paris where they are today.

After the Second World War, however, the distinguished English philosopher, Bertrand Russell, wrote: 'The dictatorships of Russia and Germany (especially the latter) are in part an outcome of Rousseau's teaching.' Che Guevara carried a copy of *The Social Contract* with him on his campaigns. It continues to inspire and to anger in almost equal proportions.

In brief, it is a book that cannot be ignored and I believe it is particularly relevant to your debates and negotiations within the Students' League of Nations. Indeed, it could become the SUN handbook, as in some ways it has become the United Nations handbook, because in *The Social Contract* Rousseau is trying to address the fundamental question: 'How can people live together in security and harmony without surrendering too much individual freedom?' We are back to the airport security check in Miami.

Does the process of civilization require human beings to give up the individual freedom that they enjoyed in their natural state (as hunter-gatherers, if you like) to spend their lives 'in chains' as the slaves of dictators, princes or mobs? As we look around us today, we may observe fewer dictators, fewer princes and fewer mobs than there were in the 18th century, but we still see many political obstacles that prevent ordinary, decent people from living fulfilled lives in acceptable health and security.

Rousseau poses the challenge as follows:

'To find a form of association which may defend and protect with the whole force of the community the person and property of every associate, and by means of which each, coalescing with all, may nevertheless obey only himself, and remain as free as before.' (I,6)

The answer, he says, lies in a 'social contract' which requires that:

'Each of us puts in common his person and his whole power under the supreme direction of the general will; and in return we receive every member as an indivisible part of the whole.' (I,6)

In other words, each individual must be prepared to give up a measure of individual liberty in order to achieve the more significant right of civil liberty. The justification for this, says Rousseau, is not only that we will sleep more soundly at night, but that human beings will achieve their proper dignity in behaving in this way. This is perhaps the most powerful passage in the whole book and I want to quote it complete because you will immediately recognize in so many political situations today – kidnapping, suicide bombing, corruption and torture – the very opposite of what Rousseau is describing:

> 'The passage from the state of nature to the civil state produces in man a very remarkable change, by substituting in his conduct justice for instinct, and by giving his actions the moral quality that they previously lacked. It is only when the voice of duty succeeds physical impulse, and law succeeds appetite, that man, who 'til then had regarded only himself, sees that he is obliged to act on other principles, and to consult his reason before listening to his inclinations. Although, in this state, he is deprived of many advantages that he derives from nature, he acquires equally great ones in return; his faculties are exercised and ennobled; his whole soul is exalted to such a degree that… he ought to bless without ceasing the happy moment that released him from it for ever, and transformed him from a stupid and ignorant animal into an intelligent being and a man.' (I,8)

Rousseau's fundamental proposition then, in *The Social Contract*, is that of the 'general will'. This is not the sum of individual wills, nor the average of individual wills, nor even an acceptable compromise between individual wills, but what is deemed to be in the best interest of the society as a whole. Rousseau is fairly clear about this controversial point: there may be occasions when what the people actually decide may not coincide with what it would be rational for them to decide. The rational decision defines the general will.

Rousseau then goes on to describe what all this means in terms of government, of making and enacting laws, of religious affiliation and so on but we do not have time for that today and, in any case, it is secondary to this one, fundamental proposition of the general will.

Clearly, we have a problem because on the one hand, everyone is required to submit to what is determined to be the general will, but on the other hand, it is far from obvious who is responsible, and how, for deciding what that general will shall be. Stalin, for example, had no difficulty in determining the general will of the Soviet people – what, in the end, would be in their best interests – even though it was not evident to many of them at the time (or, indeed, since).

Many politicians are doing the same today, albeit in a more benign way. The Prime Minister of my own country, Tony Blair, whom I believe to be a decent, honourable man, has insisted on defining the general will of British citizens concerning the invasion of Iraq, despite the apparent lack of substance upon which to base it. He asks us to wait, to understand, to believe and to trust.

Rousseau realized that he had a problem. Indeed, one of the attractions of the book is the way, now and then, he takes the reader into his confidence, admitting that he cannot find an easy solution, or urging us to wait for the next chapter when all will be revealed. *The Social Contract* is a rough, thinking-out-loud document, not a smooth, polished text.

Rousseau believed that individuals, given the responsibility to legislate for the common good, will be motivated to act in the common interest but he also recognized that there will be those who will disagree and will seek to destroy the consensus. At this point our sympathy for Rousseau the Democrat begins to wobble because although he sets out to defend the rights of minorities, they have no place in his system once they organize themselves into effective oppositions.

Before proceeding further, the modern reader needs to understand that Rousseau was not imagining some abstract Utopian state and how it might be organized; he was actually imagining Geneva and how that might be organized.

In 1762, Geneva was an independent republic and it would be another 50 years before it joined Switzerland. I have an 18th century guide book which describes the Geneva Rousseau would have known in some detail: '… an ancient, large and populous town, capital of a republic of the same name near the confines of France and Switzerland… the sovereignty of this republic is lodged in the assembly of its citizens and burghers. They are jealous of their liberties.'

Rousseau was deeply proud to be a citizen of this small, independent republic (whose population in 1762 would have been fewer than 20,000) even though he had left it behind in 1756, and he signs himself in the autograph copy of the book as *'Citoyen de Genève'*. Geneva had maintained its political independence in the face of repeated threats from the surrounding dukedom of Savoie and had begun to prosper economically with the beginnings of the watch trade (Rousseau's father was a watchmaker) and international banking.

Geneva was perhaps small enough and prosperous enough for a 'general will' to exist and to be known, and for this will to be enacted through legislation by the assembly of its citizens and burghers. Indeed, in today's referendum and consensual decision-making structures, we can still see vestiges of Rousseau's thinking in contemporary Swiss politics. What upset Rousseau was his perception that the increasing power and influence of a small number of aristocratic Genevois families were undermining its precious system of democracy.

If Rousseau's political ideas are relevant only to a tiny, 18th century, independent republic why does *The Social Contract* retain its importance today? Paradoxically, what was designed for the very small has come to influence the very large because in 1919, and again in 1945, following the appalling carnage and destruction of two world wars the nations of the world came together to try to determine a global 'general will':

> 'We the peoples of the United Nations determined to save succeeding generations from the scourge of war, which twice in our lifetime has brought untold sorrow to mankind... ' (Charter of the United Nations)

In particular, the fact that human beings now possessed nuclear weapons that could destroy all life on the planet brought a new and powerful focus to the search for a general will which was realized through

- the formation of the United Nations as an organization

- the General Assembly of the UN which brings together all the nations of the world (currently 191)

- the powers given to its Security Council to enforce the 'general will'

- the Universal Declaration of Human Rights which contains the formal expression of that 'general will'

and it cannot be coincidental that Article 1 of the Universal Declaration is written in language that seems to come straight from *The Social Contract*:

> 'All human beings are born free and equal in dignity and rights. They are endowed with reason and conscience and should act towards one another in a spirit of brotherhood.'

So, *honorables délégués*, the building you are meeting in, the organization that it houses and the work you are engaged in are all derived from this remarkable man, Jean-Jacques Rousseau. *The Social Contract* inspires, it infuriates, it provokes and it challenges, and it will deserve to be read just as long as anyone is interested in that most fundamental of questions: How can different people come together to live acceptable lives in harmony?

Let me end with a postscript that links Rousseau, rather sadly, to the International School of Geneva. A year after *The Social Contract* was published, the Republic of Geneva made known its official reply. It was written by the Procureur Général, Jean-Robert Tronchin, and was entitled *Lettres Ecrites de la Compagne* (letters written from the countryside).

Rousseau could not resist replying to this attack which he did in 1764 in *Lettres Ecrites de la Montagne* (he was living in the Jura at the time) in which he accused the Geneva authorities of corruption, so angering them that he was forced to flee to seek temporary asylum, eventually in England.

Tronchin lived in the château at La Grande Boissiere (which was then in the countryside!) and so from what is now the International School of Geneva was launched the attack that forced Rousseau to give up what he treasured most: his citizenship of Geneva.

To read *The Social Contract* is a struggle, but it is a worthwhile struggle which I hope you will undertake. After all, the real struggle is learning to live together in peace and harmony with people who are different from ourselves and that is precisely the issue that Rousseau helps us to understand better.

50th anniversary of the founding of the Student United Nations
Geneva, Switzerland, December 2003

"National education has always contained an international dimension but the need to 'think globally' introduces new concepts and stimulates new interpretations of previous learning."

In this article I reflect on 15 years' engagement with international education. I return to my first writing on the subject and suggest that there are three progressive stages in becoming a global citizen: international understanding, global understanding and global citizenship. I then use the example of a remarkable lady to illustrate some of the practical challenges faced by internationally-minded teachers.

Learning some lessons about international education

It is a great pleasure to be back in Scandinavia and a particular pleasure to be in Sweden. I have very special memories of previous meetings in Iceland and Denmark so thank you for inviting me once again to join you at your conference.

Not surprisingly, you find me in retrospective mood. At the end of this month I shall have been director general of the IBO for six years (which means it is now impossible to blame anyone else!) but quite soon after that – 1st January to be exact – I shall be handing over to my successor.

Describing international education

It is a good moment, therefore, to look back but instead of asking the obvious question, "What have I achieved?" I am going to ask the more intriguing question, "What have I learned?" and in particular, "What have I learned about international education?" After all, that is our core business; it is the 'I' in IBO and we put it at the heart of our mission when we state that it is through 'challenging programmes of international education' that we expect to develop those inquiring, knowledgeable, caring, active and compassionate life-long learners.

I am going to start back in 1991, long before I joined the IBO. I had been appointed director general of the International School of Geneva which (it would claim from time to time) had practically invented international education! Anyway, that did not stop me setting up a small working group to try to reach a consensus, and then publish a set of principles, on an international education. In the end, it turned out rather well, and the work we did has been widely quoted, but I shall never forget the first meeting when the most articulate member of the group said, "I really don't know what we are doing here. There is nothing special about international education: it is simply a good education that everyone should have."

Fifteen years later, I agree and I disagree. I agree that everyone should have the opportunity to benefit from an international education. I do not agree that it is 'simply a good education' because I believe it has some distinctive elements which do not happen by chance; they need deliberate planning. Anyway, my first opportunity to write on the subject (and remember that for the previous 25 years I had worked in the state system of education in Britain) came in 1995 and here are the six characteristics of international education that I thought important:

- Communication: knowing how to access information

- Negotiation: the skill of persuading people to compromise or change their minds

- Political awareness: understanding why nations have particular priorities

- Cultural understanding: recognizing that different groups have different mindsets

- Global issues: studying problems that impact across nations

- Criteria for truth: how do we judge what is right or wrong?

Step 1: International awareness

Looking back, I am quite pleased with that list – it was not a bad first try – but I now find it rather muddled and I will explain why in a moment. First, I want to mention what I deliberately left out which included teaching groups of different nationalities, studying the history, geography and customs of other countries, arranging exchanges with foreign schools and having a strong modern languages department, though I did add that each of those might help.

Let me explain why I chose to exclude 'teaching groups of different nationalities' which many would regard as a key feature of international education. I cannot agree. It may be a key feature of international *schools* but I see no reason at all why international *education* should be confined to, or defined by, international schools. Its relevance is much wider than that.

I now realize that, in that early list, I was struggling to make sense of three different levels of international education. The first is what I now call 'international awareness'. This means being conscious of other nationalities for very practical reasons: you may go on holiday to a different country or buy property there; you might want to do business there, or work in a mixed-nationality team; there is a possibility your children will live there and your grandchildren speak their language, not yours. For all those reasons you will want to know about that country's location, its history, its culture and its language.

International awareness in education has become an important area of concern for politicians. Former US Secretary of Education, Richard Riley, expressed this in 2000 when he said:

'I strongly believe that the growth of democracy, economic prosperity and economic stability throughout the world is linked to the advance of education. This is one of the strongest reasons why the United States should have an active and strong international education agenda.'

More recently, the Australian Federal Minister of Education, Brendan Nelson, wrote of the importance of:

'encouraging all Australian students to study abroad, to study an internationally relevant curriculum and to learn other languages so as to engage in a dynamic global workforce.'

And there are very few developed countries that are not measuring their education systems against those in other countries, for example using PISA (Programme for International Student Assessment) which surveys every three years the knowledge and skills of 15-year old students in the principal industrialized countries. Indeed, to become part of PISA is a political aspiration of many developing countries.

So, an early piece of my learning about international education was to put international awareness on the first step on the ladder. Yes: it *is* encouraged by appropriate history and geography programmes, by a vibrant modern languages department, teacher and student exchanges and by all kinds of other international experiences including the famous five Fs: food, festivals, folklore, fashion and famous people.

But, for me, it is only the first step on the ladder.

Step 2: Global awareness

The next step was described by a former UK Secretary of State for Education who was a strong supporter of the IB in its early days, Shirley Williams, now Baroness Williams. Back in 1981 at an IB conference of governments she suggested that:

'The world is becoming like scorpions in a bottle, who have learned in a very short time that they either live together or that they mortally wound one another. For we deal, of course, with a situation which is very new: where the luxury of being able to vent national feelings, xenophobia, national hatred, racial prejudice and so forth, is one that has only recently come into question; and where much of the education system in all countries, including our own, has simply not taken on board sufficiently the international dimension and the degree of international interdependence to which we are now heir.'

Had she been writing today, I believe she would use the word 'globalization' because that is what she is talking about – international interdependence on a multilateral scale – and, interestingly, she is discussing it not in terms of communication or economics, not even in terms of politics, but in the context of ethics. How are we all going to behave as the world becomes like a bottle and how is education going to help us to behave?

Shirley Williams provides the second rung of my ladder which I shall call 'global awareness', the recognition that we are now all globally interconnected. The idea is hardly new, and it is interesting to find on the internet the famous (almost clichéd) lines of the 16th century poet, John Donne:

> 'Any man's death diminishes me because I am involved in mankind and therefore never send to know for whom the bell tolls; it tolls for thee.'

linked to two very modern, global disasters, the events of 9/11 and the tsunami catastrophe.

Looking back at my original list which I criticized as muddled, I can select three items which are related to the concept of global awareness. The first is **communication** and at the time I was making the point that in the modern world, very little can be concealed or kept confidential. Today I would add that the internet puts the power of communication into the hands of people who no longer need to be part of a recognized institution to make use of it. That applies to the wealth-creating entrepreneur who may be anywhere in the world and the same applies to the terrorist.

I called the second point **political awareness** and by it I mean understanding why nations behave as they do. Why has the United States refused to sign up to the Kyoto Protocol on atmospheric pollution; why has the government of Bosnia taken so long to arrest suspected war criminals; why does Japan keep asking to resume its whaling operations; why has Iran restarted its uranium enrichment programme? Are they all being deliberately perverse or are there more complex reasons that the globally aware person should understand? Politics has been defined as the art of the possible and I sometimes think there is a lack of understanding amongst international educators about what is politically possible in certain situations; what is reasonable to expect of politicians and governments in real-life situations. My third point was a rather obvious one and simply suggested that what I am calling global awareness is likely to be encouraged by a study of **global issues** that cross national frontiers, which might include issues of health, the environment, poverty, conflict resolution, and so on. Such issues feature strongly in the IB Primary Years and Middle Years programmes, but they are sometimes hard to find in the Diploma Programme.

Professor Howard Gardner has written:

'The trends of globalization – the unprecedented and unpredictable movement of human beings, capital, information and cultural life forms – need to be understood by the young persons who are and will always inhabit a global community. Some of the system will become manifest through the media; but many other facets – for example, the operation of worldwide markets – will need to be taught in a more formal manner.'

In *Globalization. Culture and Education in the New Millennium*
M. M. Suarez-Orozco & D. B. Qin-Hilliard (Eds)
Berkeley: University of California Press, 2004

The distinguished American journalist, Thomas Friedman, in his best seller *The World is Flat* (Allen Lane, 2005) has described how a number of factors have come together in the past decade to create unprecedented opportunities around the globe for people who have hitherto been excluded from participation. These factors include the collapse of the Soviet Union and its state-controlled economy, access to the internet and the supportive interconnectivity of software and these, in turn, have led to new sets of business practices and skills that have released the energy and ideas of millions of new participants, particularly in India and China. At the same time they threaten the traditional economic prosperity of millions of others, not least in the United States where, in Friedman's view, the quality of education is too poor to allow people to compete on what is slowly becoming a more level playing field.

Education, insists Friedman, is the most effective leveller of the playing field.

'Jobs are going to go where the best educated workforce is with the most competitive infrastructure and environment for creativity and supportive government.'

So, I have learned that to be on the first rung of the ladder of international education is not enough. The best educated workforce is no longer just internationally aware. It has an understanding of the major influences that have consigned the concepts of the independent nation state, national company and national economy to the history books. I have learned that students need to be globally aware.

Step 3: The global citizen

There are three remaining items on that original list which are:

- Understanding criteria for truth

- Cultural understanding

- Skills of negotiation

and these are going to take me up to the third level of my ladder where I learn what it means to be a 'global citizen'.

Sometime last year, I received a pamphlet from Washington International School (WIS) entitled 'Educating the Global Citizen'. Let me quote:

> 'Educating global citizens means much more than exposure to many nationalities, learning about multiple cultures, or even immersion in other languages. It requires giving students the outlook and skills that equip them with mental flexibility and a basic respect for perspectives other than their own.

> 'A global citizen is one who seeks out a range of views and perspectives when solving problems. He or she does not "tolerate" or "accept" cultural difference or viewpoints, since these words implicitly place the speaker at the centre of what is acceptable and right. Global citizens proactively seek out those who have backgrounds that are different from their own, examine ideas that challenge their own and then enjoy the complexity.

> 'A global citizen examines and respects differences, and evaluates them critically. He or she does not passively accept all ideas or philosophies. Engagement – in thought, in discussion, in active learning – is the basis for global citizenship.'

I have quoted that at some length because it is one of the best descriptions I have seen of the qualities of the global citizen. I also believe that there is considerable overlap with the three items that I selected from my own list.

For example, you will have noticed the emphasis on active learning in the WIS statement: 'seeks out', 'examines', 'evaluates', 'mental flexibility', 'proactive' and so on. At the heart of global citizenship is a lively mind but a mind that will be operating within boundaries defined by truth and falsehood. The sky is not the limit when it comes to exercising the intellect: our **concept of truth** will define the limits and that will need refocusing depending on the particular area of knowledge – scientific, mathematical, artistic, literary, ethical, religious and so on. That is why I have learned to appreciate the value of the IB's Theory of Knowledge course in the education of the global citizen.

I also have learned a lot about the importance of **culture** (the 'software of the mind') in making sense of the way other people behave. During the past 15 years I have frequently been required to surrender my autonomy, my competence, even part of my personality by speaking someone else's language. But since I am a native English speaker it happens more frequently that the other person is required to use mine. I have learned something about the different symbols and rituals that characterize life in Switzerland and I can now understand that nation's fear of being gobbled up into a large, anonymous European Union. However, understanding these issues does not in any way imply approval and I will return to that in a moment.

But let me not exaggerate: living in international Geneva is not a hugely different experience from living in any other cosmopolitan city. How would the IB get on, I wonder, if we moved our curriculum and assessment centre to Damascus? After all, we are supposed to be international, it would certainly be cheaper than Britain and Syria is in the same IBO region as Cardiff, Geneva and Stockholm. How would the IB get on, I wonder, if my successor were not American, but Chinese, educated exclusively in China? I seriously doubt whether the organization could sustain either culture shock because, in the end, much of what we do is not really international, it has been developed from a very influential Western humanist tradition of learning.

So another thing I have learned about international education is that it is very rarely truly international. To take just one example, what view do we have of collaborative working which is an important feature of many non-Western cultures? We seem to encourage it in the classroom and then punish it in the examination hall. How do we reconcile a spirit of inquiry with a patriarchal culture that puts a high premium on received wisdom and rote learning? How can a secular curriculum be adopted in a country where religious faith, rather than empirical observation, defines the limits of truth? *Is it possible to be a free-thinking individual, perhaps perceived as amoral, in a culture where the rules and rituals are unconditionally accepted and rigorously adhered to?*

That last question is not mine, but was asked by a young Jordanian IB coordinator during a presentation at a regional conference in Oman in 1999. I was so impressed by the clarity with which she explained her cultural dilemma that I asked for a copy and I have kept it ever since. There is no simple answer here and the best we can do is to be honest about what the IB is and what it is not, to try slowly but deliberately, to widen its international perspective and to help our students to understand that there are very different ways of looking at the same world.

Cultural understanding does not imply infinite cultural tolerance; I said I would return to this point. Cultures which encourage corruption, and censorship and deny basic human rights, particularly those of women, are undesirable and the global citizen should be prepared to say so and to engage in debate to persuade others of this point of view. That is why I have listed the art of **negotiation** as an essential skill. I listened recently to a fascinating interview with the conductor, Daniel Barenboim, who had brought his mixed Arab-Israeli orchestra to London (it is called the East-Western Divan Orchestra). He was asked if the different groups brought their political differences into their work as musicians. Yes, he said, they often argued passionately but three special factors pertain:

1. no one is allowed to join the orchestra if they believe that the Middle East problem requires a military solution

2. they all recognize that the success of a symphony orchestra requires everyone to support everyone else; it is a collaborative effort or it is nothing

3. the shared commitment to making music provides a bond that allows differences to be explored without a threat to mutual respect.

He described it as follows: "The opportunity to listen to the narrative of others – their story – to challenge it and to have them challenge yours." But that common thread of music (or whatever – it has been called a 'thread of affiliation') is an essential starting point.

Barenboim's word 'challenge' makes me think that my choice of the term 'negotiate' was right. It is not just a question of listening, understanding and then disagreeing. That achieves nothing. It is rather taking up the challenge to seek an agreement which will often be in the form of a compromise. And that is the process that negotiation describes.

We have arrived at the third rung on the ladder: we have moved from the student who is internationally aware, to one who is globally aware to one who is a true global citizen, the person who has the necessary intellectual skills, the cultural understanding and both the ability and the attitude to shift another person's position as well as their own. For me, citizenship implies action.

Step 4: Making it happen

A moment ago I said that the International School of Geneva sometimes claims to have invented international education. That is not quite as arrogant as it seems because in 1948, 20 years before the IB, the director of the school, an extraordinary lady called Marie-Thérèse Maurette, wrote a handbook for UNESCO which is still to be found in their archives in Paris. It was entitled *Techniques d'education pour la paix. Existent-elles?* In English we might say *Is there a way of teaching for peace?* It is a very special document and I am going to use it to illustrate my final point today.

Perhaps the most important thing I have learned about international education is that it does not happen by chance, by some kind of mysterious osmosis. It is not caught; it is taught. In order to make this point I want, quite deliberately, to take you away from the IB with which you are so familiar and present you with Mme Maurette's views which will be quite new.

First of all, Maurette is quite sceptical about the role played by friendships. Rubbing shoulders certainly helps, she says, but it is not enough. So she starts by insisting on certain values. For example, to insult someone's nationality or race is, in her words, *"le crime des crimes"* but at the same time, she urges her teachers to play down the whole concept of nationality, either as a source of pride or of pity. Let's avoid all sentimentality, she says.

She then argues the case for a new kind of geography which puts the students into contact with the whole world before they ever see a map of their own country. Individual maps are hopelessly misleading, she says, so the Swiss have no idea that the delta of the River Ganges is as large as Switzerland! The geography teacher (who conveniently happened to be her father) called the subject 'international culture' and spent much time getting each student to build up maps of the world. She had equally radical ideas about history which, she insisted, should not be taught before the age of 12 if it was to avoid becoming a gallery of dubious national heroes. For the next six years it should become world history with events in India, China, Japan and the Middle East synchronized with those in Europe. She adds rather modestly: "We have had to create our own Ronéo booklet, which is far from perfect and needs looking at by specialists."

Maurette then insists upon the acquisition of two working languages:

> *'Mais dès qu'un individu pratique vraiment les deux langues, il pratique les deux modes de pensée. En tous cas, il comprend le mode de pensée de son interlocuteur. Il n'est plus étonné et hostile. Et dès qu'il y a compréhension et familiarité, la possibilité d'entente est là: l'esprit international est né.'*

('Once someone uses two languages he uses two modes of thought. And then he understands the other person's way of thinking. He is no longer surprised or hostile. And from understanding and familiarity comes agreement: a spirit of internationalism is born.')

She then describes ways of encouraging students to keep up to date with contemporary political and economic events, and alumni of that period remember being suddenly called out of their classes to meet together to discuss some important world event, as it was happening. I suppose we would now call it 'current events' but it does not seem to play much part in the modern curriculum.

Finally, she turns to the importance of human solidarity, saying that it depends on habits of mutual support and community action and she goes on to describe the IB Creativity, Action, Service (CAS) programme 20 years before it ever happened, noting the importance of self-help projects, team sports, the student council, the school bakery run by students and so on.

I have skimmed over the surface of this unique publication because for my purpose today the details are unimportant. The important point I want to make is that the curriculum of a school can be divided roughly into three elements. There is the:

- compulsory, timetabled part of the learning in which everyone participates

- extra- or co-curriculum which is voluntary but enriches the compulsory curriculum; it is what we often remember most from our school experience

- hidden curriculum, the informal but influential rules, beliefs and attitudes that determine the school's ethos and help to transmit its values.

Mme Maurette attacks on all three curriculum fronts: compulsory, extra and hidden, realizing that each part must reinforce the others; there must be a consistency of message. But I particularly admire her courage in attacking the compulsory curriculum. For example, it's not going to be any old history course; it's going to be this special kind of history and that, of course, is her legacy to the IBO and it is no coincidence that the IB Diploma Programme grew out of a syllabus and an examination called Contemporary World History.

But the IB can only do so much and within each element of the curriculum, and particularly in creating the hidden curriculum that determines the school's values, it will be the teachers and the administrators who have an overwhelming influence. The research of my colleagues at the University of Bath, Dr Mary Hayden and Professor Jeff Thompson, has confirmed that in the eyes of students, teachers and alumni who have experienced an international education, the international-mindedness of their teachers and a management regime value-consistent with an institutional international philosophy are two essential ingredients.

It is time to sum up. I have tried to trace a path within international education from being internationally aware, to being globally aware to being a truly global citizen. I do not believe that international education is simplistically synonymous with 'a high quality education', nor do I believe that it happens by chance. So let me end by paying tribute to all of you here today who work so hard to help us to design international programmes and then use them to create international education in all your different schools.

Conference of Nordic IB Schools, Stockholm, Sweden, September 2005